VIJAYSHREE R

The Five Sacred Expressions of Love

The Bhagavad Gita's Guide to Deepening Connection, Compassion, and Joy in Every Relationship

First published by Shree's Essencia 2025

All illustrations in this book were generated with the assistance of AI tools. The people and scenes depicted are symbolic and illustrative, not exact portrayals of real individuals.

The stories in this book are inspired by the dynamics of Indian families and the universal experiences of love, growth, and togetherness. They draw upon the timeless wisdom of the Bhagavad Gita to offer insights into daily life and relationships.

Coming from a large joint family and having witnessed the joys and challenges of close relationships, I've drawn from real experiences to craft these stories as a heartfelt tribute to the love and lessons our family has shared.

First edition

ISBN: 978-93-344-5163-4

This book was professionally typeset on Reedsy.
Find out more at reedsy.com

To my beloved family —
who taught me the meaning of patience, forgiveness, and selfless love,
who shared laughter, tears, and countless quiet moments,
and whose lives reflect the sacred rhythm of togetherness.
This is for the hearts that held me,
for the hands that guided me,
and for the souls that inspired me to live with compassion, devotion, and integrity.
This book is my humble offering,
a reflection of the timeless teachings that shaped our journey together.
-Vijayshree

"The heart that gives with purity
and the mind that reflects with clarity
are the gateways to love, harmony, and truth.
In every act, in every word, in every silence,
the divine whispers its guidance,
teaching us how to live, forgive, and connect."
— Inspired by the Bhagavad Gita

—Vijayshree Ratanparkhe

Contents

	Foreword	iii
	Preface	v
	Prologue	1
	Introduction	2
1	Healing the Heart: Understanding the Spiritual Blocks in...	13
2	Day 1: The Power of Gratitude	19
3	Day 2: The Power of Listening	26
4	Day 3: Recognizing Sacred Expressions of Love	34
5	Day 4: Being Fully Present	50
6	Day 5: Empathy Check-In	57
7	Day 6: Acts of Selfless Love	65
8	Day 7: The Power of Self-Reflection	72
9	Day 8: Expressing Appreciation	80
10	Day 9: Observing Without Judgment	87
11	Day 10: Forgiveness and Letting Go	95
12	Day 11: Understanding Needs Through Sacred Expressions of...	102
13	Day 12: Respecting Boundaries	109
14	Day 13: Resolving Conflict with Discernment and Steadiness	116
15	Day 14: Cultivating Gratitude with Devotion	123
16	Day 15: Divine Expressions of Love in Action	131
17	Day 16: Practicing Non-Judgmental Awareness	146

18 Day 17: Apology and Forgiveness 154
19 Day 18: Self-Compassion 162
20 Day 19: Honest Sharing 169
21 Day 20: Celebrating Sacred Connections 175
22 Day 21: Reflection on Growth 182
23 Glossary of Key Terms and Concepts 189
24 Conclusion 193
Epilogue 202
Afterword 203
About the Author 205
Also by Vijayshree R 207

Foreword

Life's deepest lessons often come through our relationships — they mirror our strengths, vulnerabilities, attachments, and capacity to love. I have had the blessing of witnessing this firsthand while conducting a heartfelt workshop, where participants explored the sacred expressions of love inspired by the Bhagavad Gita. Each person brought their unique story, their joys, their struggles, and their sincere desire to connect with themselves and others in a meaningful way.

Through those sessions, I realized how profoundly the Gita's wisdom can transform our everyday interactions. It teaches us to be fully present, to act with empathy, to give selflessly, and to honor the divine spark in everyone we meet. Observing participants embody these principles, even in small ways, was a humbling and inspiring experience. I am deeply grateful to each individual who brought their openness, trust, and curiosity to the workshop — your presence enriched this learning and made the experience alive.

This book is the next step in that journey, guided by divine inspiration. It captures the practical applications of timeless wisdom, offering readers a pathway to create harmony, deepen connections, and honor the divine in themselves and in others. It is both a guide and an invitation — to approach relationships with awareness, compassion, and devotion, and to transform everyday life into a sacred practice.

— Vijayshree

Preface

This book began as a workshop — a space where people came together to explore love, connection, and the sacred bonds of family life. What emerged from those sessions was far more than I had imagined. Each interaction, reflection, and shared insight revealed the transformative power of the Bhagavad Gita's teachings.

I am grateful to everyone who participated, for your trust, openness, and willingness to explore these truths. Through divine guidance, what was once a workshop has now become a book — a bridge between lived experience and timeless wisdom. The guidance shared here is not theoretical; it comes from observing, practicing, and learning alongside others, and from applying these principles in my own life within the rich dynamics of a joint family.

Here, you will find practical guidance drawn from Satya (Truthful Speech), Seva (Selfless Service), Sangha (Sacred Presence), Sparsha (Respectful Connection), Dana (Heartful Offering), and the many virtues illuminated in the Gita. My hope is that these pages inspire you to bring awareness, compassion, and selfless love into your relationships, cultivating harmony, understanding, and inner peace. May this book serve as a companion on your own journey of mindful, heart-centered living.

— Vijayshree

Prologue

Life in a joint family is a rich tapestry of love, laughter, challenge, and learning. Every relationship is a teacher, every interaction an opportunity to practice presence, patience, and understanding. Conducting the workshop allowed me to witness this living wisdom in action — seeing people embrace reflection, compassion, and selfless love in their own lives. It reminded me that the lessons of the heart often emerge in the smallest moments: a kind word, a thoughtful gesture, a willingness to listen, or the courage to forgive.

The Bhagavad Gita became my guide throughout this journey. Its teachings offered ways to listen deeply, act with intention, forgive without attachment, and love unconditionally. The reflections, exercises, and insights shared in this book are drawn from those experiences — a tapestry of lived practice and divine guidance. They are meant to help readers cultivate meaningful connections, heal old wounds, and embrace the sacredness inherent in every relationship, no matter how ordinary it may seem.

— Vijayshree

Introduction

The Story of Sita and the Six Heart Blocks

Once upon a time, in a peaceful town surrounded by nature's beauty, there lived a warm-hearted woman named **Sita**. She had a loving family — her husband **Raj**, their young daughter **Avantika**, and her parents **Lalitha** and **Raghav**.

From the outside, everything seemed perfect. Yet Sita often felt a quiet emptiness — a sense of distance even amidst love.

One day, as she sat in her garden under a neem tree, reflecting on her restlessness, an elderly sage named **Acharya** walked by. Known for his deep understanding of the **Bhagavad Gita**, Acharya was revered for helping people rediscover peace in their hearts.

Sita greeted him and shared her pain:

"Acharya, I have love in my life, yet I feel disconnected—from Raj, from my parents, and even from myself. Sometimes we laugh, and everything feels fine; at other times, I feel unseen, unheard, or angry."

Acharya smiled gently. "My child, the Gita says that the heart is like a mirror — naturally clear, but covered by the dust of attachment and desire. When this dust settles, love shines effortlessly. Let me tell you about the **six inner blocks** that cloud love's natural flow."

The Six Heart Blocks

"Imagine your heart as a sacred river," Acharya began.

"When it flows freely, it reflects divine beauty and peace. But when obstacles arise — fear, anger, or ego — the waters become turbulent. These are the **six heart blocks** every seeker must purify to experience love as the Gita teaches — pure, selfless, and divine."

1. The Fear of Vulnerability — Opening the Heart with Trust (Śraddhā)

"Do you remember when you were afraid to express your feelings to Raj?" asked Acharya.

"You hid your fears, believing that showing your uncertainty would make you appear weak."

Sita nodded.

"Fear of vulnerability," said Acharya, "is the armor of the ego. But in truth, love requires **śraddhā** — trust and faith. When you open your heart without fear, you align with divine courage. The Gita reminds us, *'One who has faith, whose heart is devoted, and who has mastered doubt, attains peace.'* (4.39)

True intimacy begins when you allow your heart to be seen."

2. The Weight of Unresolved Anger — Releasing through Compassion (Karunā)

"Anger, when held, becomes poison," said Acharya softly.

"You once felt resentment toward your mother, Lalitha, for her harsh words, didn't you?"

Sita sighed. "Yes, I carried it for so long."

"Anger arises when expectations clash with attachment," he explained. "The Gita teaches us to act from **karunā**, compassion. *'Freed from anger and attachment, such a person attains peace.'* (5.26)

When you forgive, you don't excuse others — you free your own heart to love again."

3. Attachment to Material Things — Remembering True Wealth (Santosha)

"Sometimes," said Acharya, "our hearts seek satisfaction in possessions or recognition, forgetting that joy lies within."

He looked at Sita kindly. "You compared your home and life with others, didn't you?"

She lowered her eyes. "Yes. I thought more would make me happier."

Acharya nodded. "The Gita calls this **moha** — delusion born of desire. *'When a person gives up all desires born of the mind and is content in the Self alone, they attain lasting peace.'* (2.55)

Happiness is not in having more, but in **being more present** — in gratitude and love."

4. The Ego and Selfishness — Surrendering through Seva (Selfless Action)

"Ego whispers, 'I first.' But love says, 'We together,'" Acharya smiled.

"When you felt Raj was ignoring your needs, did you pause to see his exhaustion?"

Sita looked surprised. "No, I assumed he didn't care."

"The ego," Acharya continued, "creates separation. But the Gita guides us toward **seva** — selfless service. *'Perform your duty without attachment, and by doing so, you reach the Supreme.'* (3.19)

When you serve with love, the 'I' dissolves, and oneness blossoms. True love is not about being right — it's about being kind."

5. The Burden of Unforgiveness — Letting Go with Wisdom (Viveka)

"Unforgiveness is a heavy stone on the heart," Acharya said. "You once held onto your father's hurtful words, didn't you?"

Sita nodded slowly.

"Forgiveness doesn't mean forgetting," said Acharya. "It means seeing with **viveka** — discernment. The Gita reminds us, *'The wise see with equal vision — a learned sage, a cow, an elephant, even a dog or an outcaste.'* (5.18)

When you see all souls as divine, judgment melts into understanding. Forgiveness purifies the heart, allowing love to flow again."

6. The Strain of Misguided Expectations — Cultivating Acceptance (Samatvam)

"Expectations are like invisible threads," Acharya explained. "We tie them around others and feel pain when they don't move as we wish."

Sita reflected. "Yes, I often expect Raj or Avantika to know what I need without saying it."

"The Gita calls this attachment to results," he said. "Practice **samatvam** — evenness of mind. *'Perform your duty with balance, abandoning all attachment to success or failure.'* (2.48)

When you communicate clearly and accept others as they are, you align with divine harmony."

Moral of the Story — The Path of Heart Purification

Acharya looked at her gently.

"My child, these six blocks — fear, anger, attachment, ego, unforgiveness, and expectation — are the clouds that veil divine love. The Gita teaches that by cultivating **faith, compassion, contentment, service, wisdom, and balance**, the heart becomes pure once again."

Sita smiled softly. "I want to live this truth. I want to free my heart."

"Then begin," said Acharya. "Each act of love, done in awareness and devotion, is a step toward the Divine. Love is not something we receive; it is what we become."

Invitation to Heal and Transform

As Sita's heart lightened, she felt ready to walk the path of **bhakti**, love in action. She shared her reflections with Raj, Avantika, Lalitha, and Raghav, and together, they decided to live these principles in daily life.

They practiced **truthful speech (Satya)**, **selfless service (Seva)**, **mindful presence (Sangha)**, **compassionate connection (Sparsha)**, and **heartful giving (Dana)** — the five sacred expressions of love that blossom from a pure heart.

In time, their home became a living temple of love and awareness. The family learned that the greatest relationship is the one that mirrors the relationship between the soul and the Divine.

And so, their story became a timeless lesson — that the *Bhagavad Gita's wisdom is not only about duty or detachment, but about love that uplifts, unites, and transforms.*

The End.

* * *

Why You Should Read The 21-Day Relationship Transformation Journey Guided by the Bhagavad Gita

Are you ready to deepen your relationships and transform how you connect with the people you love?

This 21-day journey, guided by the timeless wisdom of the Bhagavad Gita, will lead you through a process of connection, compassion, and spiritual growth.

Rooted in the Gita's teachings on self-awareness, selfless action, and emotional balance, this book helps you cultivate understanding, faith, and harmony in your relationships.

Here's why this book is essential for fostering deeper, more meaningful connections and lasting well-being.

Connection and Conscious Awareness

At the heart of every meaningful relationship is awareness — awareness of the self, of others, and of the divine presence within all.

The Bhagavad Gita teaches that when we understand our inner nature (Swadharma) and act with compassion (Karunā) and discernment (Viveka), our relationships become sacred expressions of love.

In today's fast-paced world, it's easy to overlook the importance of mindful presence and genuine connection.

This book helps you rediscover the power of conscious awareness, empathy, and divine-centered understanding, grounded in the Gita's principles of mindfulness in action (Karma Yoga) and love as devotion (Bhakti Yoga).

Expressing Love Through the Divine Path

We often express love in ways that come naturally to us, yet may not fully align with how others experience it. The Bhagavad Gita invites us to move beyond self-centered expression and cultivate Nishkama Karma — selfless love and service without attachment to results.

By learning to understand and honor the spiritual needs and emotions of others, we awaken the ability to love without conditions or expectations.

This book guides you to express love through the Gita's path of devotion (Bhakti), selfless service (Seva), truthful speech (Satya), mindful presence (Sankalpa), and heartful giving (Dana) — the sacred ways of divine connection.

The Five Sacred Expressions of Love

Every soul expresses and receives love in unique ways. The Bhagavad Gita teaches that love is not merely an emotion, but an expression of our divine nature — selfless, truthful, and pure. When guided by spiritual awareness, our relationships become sacred paths of connection and service.

Through this book, you'll explore the Five Sacred Expressions of Love, inspired directly by the teachings of the Gita:

- **Satya (Truthful Expression)** — Speaking with honesty, kindness, and integrity. True love thrives on truth that uplifts, never wounds.
- **Seva (Selfless Service)** — Expressing love through action and care, serving others without expectation or attachment.
- **Sparsha (Loving Presence)** — Offering your full attention, empathy, and gentle awareness — being present with heart and soul.
- **Dana (Heartful Giving)** — Giving freely of your time, affection, and support, not for reward but from joy and compassion.
- **Bhakti (Devotional Love)** — Seeing every relationship as sacred; offering your love, forgiveness, and gratitude to the Divine through others.

When these five sacred expressions flow together, relationships become a form of yoga — union.

As the Gita reminds us:

"The wise see with equal vision — the Divine present in every being." (5.18)

Through this awareness, you learn to love not only others, but also the Divine reflected in them.

Holistic Healing Through Connection

This book is not just about communication — it is about healing the heart. Through daily reflection, compassion, and forgiveness, you will dissolve the inner blocks that prevent love from flowing freely.

The Gita teaches that peace begins within:

"One who has conquered the mind finds peace within the Self; such a person is steadfast in heat and cold, in pleasure and pain." (6.7)

By practicing non-judgment, patience, and empathy, you will cultivate harmony within yourself and in your relationships, awakening the divine quality of Samatvam — inner balance and equanimity.

Transformational Growth in Relationships

Whether it's with a partner, parent, child, or friend, this journey will help you release old patterns of attachment, misunderstanding, and hurt. The Bhagavad Gita teaches the art of transformation through awareness, self-discipline, and surrender.

Through guided reflections and practices, you'll learn to:

- Recognize the root of emotional reactions
- Transform expectation into acceptance
- Replace blame with understanding
- Celebrate love as a form of divine energy, not mere emotion

This transformation is inspired by the Gita's wisdom:

"Perform your duty without attachment; remain balanced in success and failure — this evenness is called Yoga." (2.48)

Practical Application of Love and Spiritual Principles

This book is not theoretical — it is a daily spiritual practice. Guided by the Bhagavad Gita's teachings, you will engage in mindful exercises such as:

- Expressing gratitude (Kritajñatā)
- Practicing forgiveness (Kshamā)
- Listening with presence (Shraddhā)
- Serving with love (Seva)
- Offering your actions to the Divine (Ishvara Arpana Buddhi)

These daily practices will help you experience real transformation in how you communicate, love, and serve others.

Restoration of Emotional Balance

Emotions can be powerful guides or obstacles — the Gita calls this the dance of the three gunas (sattva, rajas, tamas). Through awareness and spiritual discipline, you will learn to observe emotions without being controlled by them.

Whether it's setting healthy boundaries, releasing judgment, or expressing needs with clarity, this book helps you develop emotional steadiness (Sthitaprajna) — a balanced state of mind that responds, not reacts.

"When the mind is steady and free from desires, like a lamp in a windless place, the yogi rests in union with the Divine." (6.19)

This inner peace becomes the foundation for all harmonious relationships.

Why You Should Read This Book

- **Personal Transformation** – Let go of old emotional patterns and rediscover your inner peace through faith (Śraddhā), devotion (Bhakti), and balance (Samatvam).
- **Empowerment Through Wisdom** – Learn practical spiritual tools from the Bhagavad Gita to manage emotions, cultivate awareness, and face life's challenges with courage and grace.
- **Healing and Emotional Resilience** – Strengthen relationships through compassion (Karunā), forgiveness (Kshamā), and understanding (Viveka).
- **Improved Relationships** – Foster deeper connection by aligning with selfless service (Seva) and divine love (Prema), leading to harmony and trust.
- **Clarity of Emotional Needs** – Reconnect with your true Self (Atman) and understand your relationships as mirrors of your spiritual journey.
- **Long-Term Impact** – Cultivate lasting transformation through

daily practice, mindfulness, and surrender, allowing the teachings of the Gita to guide your heart long after the 21 days end.

One

Healing the Heart: Understanding the Spiritual Blocks in Relationships

Release emotional pain, heal past wouns, and embrace divine love.

Recognizing the Blocks in Relationships

The challenges we face in our relationships often arise from deep-rooted **spiritual blocks** that hinder our ability to love fully and authentically. The **Bhagavad Gita** teaches that these obstacles arise from attachment (moha), desire (kāma), anger (krodha), and ignorance (avidyā), clouding our natural capacity to love with purity and selflessness.

Below is a breakdown of how these inner blocks show up in our interactions and the challenges they create:

1. Fear of Vulnerability — Lack of Faith (Śraddhā)

How Problems Arise:

Fear of being emotionally open prevents us from forming genuine bonds with others. This fear arises from insecurity, doubt, and a lack of faith — both in ourselves and in the divine presence within others.

Challenges We Face:

- Difficulty trusting others and allowing love to flow freely.
- Emotional walls that keep us from connecting deeply.
- Feelings of isolation and loneliness despite being surrounded by others.

Impact on Relationships:

- Lack of intimacy and emotional connection.
- Misunderstandings and communication breakdowns.

Gita Insight:

The Gita (4.39) reminds us that "one who has faith, whose heart is devoted, and who has mastered doubt, attains peace." When we surrender fear and trust the divine flow of life, love naturally expands.

2. Unresolved Anger and Resentment — Absence of Compassion (Karunā)

How Problems Arise:

Holding onto grudges poisons the heart and clouds judgment. Anger (krodha) arises from unfulfilled desires and expectations, as the Gita explains (2.62–63).

Challenges We Face:

- Lingering conflict and emotional distance.
- Fear of confronting uncomfortable emotions.
- Difficulty letting go of past hurts.

Impact on Relationships:

- Damage to trust and communication.
- Difficulty experiencing peace and harmony with others.

Gita Insight:

The Gita (5.26) says, "Freed from anger and attachment, such a person attains peace." Forgiveness and compassion are acts of liberation — they free both the giver and the receiver.

3. Attachments and Materialism — Forgetting Contentment (Santosha)

How Problems Arise:

When we seek happiness in possessions, status, or comparison, we lose touch with inner joy. This attachment (moha) binds us to temporary satisfaction and keeps us from lasting peace.

Challenges We Face:

- Constant comparison and dissatisfaction.

- Feelings of inadequacy or jealousy.
- Disconnection from deeper spiritual needs.

Impact on Relationships:

- Shallow connections based on validation, not love.
- A sense of emptiness despite external success.

Gita Insight:

The Gita (2.55) teaches, "When a person gives up all desires born of the mind and is content in the Self alone, he attains lasting peace." True wealth is inner fulfillment, not outer accumulation.

4. Ego and Selfishness — Absence of Selfless Service (Seva)

How Problems Arise:

When we prioritize our desires or pride over others' well-being, love becomes conditional. Ego (ahamkāra) creates separation and makes relationships transactional.

Challenges We Face:

- Difficulty listening or empathizing.
- Conflicts arising from "I first" attitudes.
- Resistance to humility or compromise.

Impact on Relationships:

- Breakdown in communication and mutual respect.
- Lack of cooperation or shared purpose.

Gita Insight:

The Gita (3.19) teaches, "Perform your duty without attachment, and by doing so, you reach the Supreme." When we act from seva — service to others as service to the Divine — ego dissolves and love unites.

5. Lack of Forgiveness — Absence of Discernment (Viveka)

How Problems Arise:

Unforgiveness binds us to the past. Without spiritual discernment (viveka), we see others only through the lens of hurt instead of the light of the soul.

Challenges We Face:

- Inability to move on from past wounds.
- Carrying resentment into new relationships.
- Fear of being hurt again.

Impact on Relationships:

- Emotional distance and repeated cycles of pain.
- Lack of trust and understanding.

Gita Insight:

The Gita (5.18) says, "The wise see with equal vision — a learned sage, a cow, an elephant, even a dog or an outcaste." Forgiveness arises from seeing the Divine equally in all, beyond the mistakes of the moment.

6. Misguided Expectations — Absence of Equanimity (Samatvam)

How Problems Arise:

When we expect others to act according to our desires, we lose balance. The Gita teaches that attachment to results (phala-āśā) creates suffering.

Challenges We Face:

- Disappointment when expectations go unmet.
- Pressure on ourselves and others to perform.
- Difficulty accepting people as they are.

Impact on Relationships:

- Strain and frustration due to unmet expectations.
- Loss of unconditional love and acceptance.

Gita Insight:

The Gita (2.48) teaches, "Perform your duty with balance, abandoning attachment to success or failure." Samatvam — evenness of mind — is the foundation of peaceful, mature love.

Breaking Free and Healing Relationships

Recognizing these blocks is the **first step toward heart purification (citta-śuddhi)**. The Bhagavad Gita shows us that healing begins not by changing others, but by transforming our own consciousness.

Through daily reflection, prayer, selfless service, and surrender, we cultivate divine virtues — **faith (śraddhā), compassion (karunā), contentment (santosha), service (seva), wisdom (viveka), and balance (samatvam)** — which dissolve the six blocks of the heart.

When these qualities blossom, relationships become sacred — not sources of need, but reflections of the Divine love that flows through all beings.

Two

Day 1: The Power of Gratitude

Theme

Reflect on Something You Appreciate About a Loved One and Express It to Them

Story: A Glass of Juice

A cool breeze wafted through the small garden as Avantika sat with her glass of juice, watching the sunlight dance on the leaves. It had been a hectic week, and her mind was full of unfinished tasks and worries. She sighed, taking a sip of her refreshing juice.

Just then, her father walked in with a quiet smile, holding a plate of her favorite cookies.

"I thought you might need a little something extra with your juice," he said, setting the plate beside her.

Avantika blinked, surprised. She hadn't even realized how much she needed this small gesture—a moment of peace in the chaos. Her father sat beside her, and his presence made her feel warm and steady.

"Thank you, Papa," she said after a moment, her voice soft but sincere. "For always noticing when I need something—even before I realize it myself."

Her father chuckled, brushing off the compliment with a wave of his hand.

"It's nothing, beta. That's what family is for."

But it wasn't "nothing" to Avantika. She realized then how often her father quietly supported her, showing love through thoughtful, small actions that she had taken for granted.

Later that evening, Avantika decided to write him a note:

"Dear Papa,

I just want to say how much I appreciate you. Your kindness and care mean the world to me, and I'm so grateful for the little things you do that make life easier and brighter. Thank you for always being there."

When she handed him the note, he looked surprised—and then deeply moved.

"Thank you, Avantika," he said, his voice thick with emotion. "It

means so much to hear that."

Reflection

Like Avantika, we often overlook the small gestures of love and care that surround us. Yet, it is these simple acts of attention and kindness that form the foundation of sacred relationships. By consciously noticing and expressing gratitude, we not only bring joy to others but also deepen our own awareness of the divine essence present in every person.

Gratitude in action reflects **Satya** (truthful, uplifting speech) and **Seva** (selfless service), transforming ordinary moments into spiritual practice and nurturing bonds of love and harmony.

Activity

Reflect

Think of someone in your life who has recently shown you kindness or support. What specific thing did they do that you truly appreciate? Reflect on how it made you feel and why it touched your heart.

Express Gratitude

Find a meaningful way to share your appreciation—write a note, send a heartfelt message, or tell them face-to-face. Be specific, acknowledging the thought, care, or devotion behind their action, just as Avantika did with her father.

Why Gratitude Matters

Gratitude is more than just saying "thank you." It is a spiritual practice that nurtures selfless love (**Prema Bhakti**), strengthens relationships, and cultivates inner peace. By acknowledging and appreciating the presence of the divine in others, we shift our mindset from attachment and expectation to detachment and selfless joy.

This practice transforms everyday interactions into acts of devotion, building not just stronger relationships but also a heart aligned with dharma and divine connection.

Guided by the Bhagavad Gita

The Bhagavad Gita teaches the importance of selfless service (**Seva**), truthful expression (**Satya**), and devotional awareness (**Bhakti**) in relationships. By practicing gratitude, we honor the divine in others, cultivating humility, empathy, and harmony.

Relevant Verses:

In **Chapter 12, Verses 13–14**, Krishna says:

> *"He who is not envious, who is a kind friend to all living beings, who is free from false ego, and who is equal in happiness and distress, who is tolerant, always satisfied, self-controlled, and engaged in devotional service with determination, and whose mind and intelligence are fixed on Me—such a devotee of Mine is very dear to Me." (BG 12.13–14)*

Relevance

Gratitude reflects the values of selfless love and devotion, which build a strong spiritual connection with those around us. By offering gratitude, we transcend personal desires and connect to the divine essence in everyone, fostering unity, peace, and deeper spiritual bonds.

Closing Thought

Just as Avantika's note brought warmth to her father's heart, your expression of gratitude can illuminate the lives of others. Notice how even small acknowledgments create ripples of love, harmony, and spiritual presence in your relationships, making ordinary moments sacred.

Three

Day 2: The Power of Listening

Theme

Listen fully with devotion and truthfulness, focusing on understanding a loved one's feelings and perspective without judgment or interruption.

Story: The Unheard Voice

Raj slumped into the chair at the dining table, his shoulders heavy with the weight of the day. Across from him, his wife, Sita, set down a steaming bowl of soup. She glanced at him, sensing the quiet storm behind his silence.

"Long day?" she asked gently, sitting down beside him.

Raj nodded but said nothing. Sita paused, resisting the urge to pepper him with questions. Instead, she waited, allowing the silence to settle.

After a moment, Raj sighed deeply.

> *"It's just... work has been overwhelming. I feel like no matter how hard I try, I'm always falling behind. And today, my manager pointed out mistakes in front of everyone. It was humiliating."*

Sita leaned forward, her gaze steady.

> *"That sounds really tough," she said softly. "It must have been frustrating and discouraging to feel called out like that."*

Raj looked up, surprised.

> *"Yeah. That's exactly how it felt. Frustrating, and like I'm not good enough."*

Sita nodded, staying silent for a moment before responding.

> *"I hear you. It's hard when you give it your all, and it still doesn't feel like enough."*

For the first time that evening, Raj smiled faintly.

> *"Thanks, Sita. Just talking about it helps. I don't know how you always know the right thing to say."*

Sita smiled back, her heart warm. She realized it wasn't about saying the "right thing"—it was about truly hearing him.

Reflection

Like Sita, we can all practice the sacred art of **śravaṇa**—deep, mindful listening. Often, people don't need advice or solutions; they simply wish to be heard and understood. When we listen with full presence, we honor the divine spark (**Paramātmā**) within the other person.

The Bhagavad Gita teaches that true communication is not about reacting, but about receiving with **shraddhā** (faithful attention) and **satya** (truthfulness). Listening with a calm, compassionate mind strengthens relationships and fosters an atmosphere of emotional safety and trust.

In the quiet of sincere listening, hearts begin to heal.

Activity

1. Set an Intention

Before engaging in conversation today, silently affirm:

> *"May I listen with patience, openness, and love."*

2. Practice Mindful Listening

- Listen without interrupting or preparing your response.
- Focus completely on the other person's words, tone, and emotions.
- Reflect what you've understood, gently affirming their feelings.

Example: "It sounds like you felt hurt when that happened."

3. Observe the Effect

Notice how the person's energy softens when they feel truly heard and seen.

Why Mindful Listening Matters

Mindful listening is an act of **seva** (service) and **bhakti** (devotion). It reminds others that they are valued and understood, not for what they do, but for who they are.

When we listen deeply, we cultivate humility—the willingness to place another's experience above our need to speak. This transforms ordinary dialogue into sacred communion.

By listening with awareness, we also calm our own restless mind, strengthening **samatvam**—the inner balance that Krishna calls the hallmark of a wise person.

> *"He who is able to withdraw the senses from their objects, as the tortoise draws its limbs within the shell, is firmly fixed in wisdom."*
> *— Bhagavad Gita 2.58*

Listening with restraint and focus mirrors this same wisdom—it is the drawing back of the mind from self-centered reaction toward compassionate understanding.

Guided by the Bhagavad Gita

Throughout the Bhagavad Gita, Krishna teaches through dialogue—and Arjuna listens with **shraddhā**, openness, and humility. This sacred conversation itself is the perfect example of divine listening: one soul opening fully to receive wisdom without resistance or judgment.

At the start of the Gita (2.11), Krishna begins to speak only after Arjuna has finished expressing his pain and confusion. Before guiding, Krishna listens. His compassionate silence allows Arjuna to unburden his heart.

Relevant Verses:

- **Chapter 2, Verse 11**
- "You speak words of wisdom, but you grieve for what is not worthy of grief. The wise lament neither for the living nor the dead."

Here, Krishna acknowledges Arjuna's pain before gently redirecting his perspective—a divine model of empathetic listening and truthful response (**satya**).

In another verse, Krishna reminds us:

- **Chapter 12, Verse 15**
- "The one whose mind is undisturbed amid misery, who remains free from desire and anger, and who is steady in both happiness and distress—such a person is dear to Me."

In **Chapter 2, Verse 70,** Krishna uses the metaphor of the ocean to illustrate inner steadiness:

> *"Just as the ocean remains undisturbed by the incessant flow of waters from rivers merging into it, likewise the sage who is unmoved despite the flow of desirable objects all around him attains peace, and not the person who strives to satisfy desires." (BG 2.70)*

By cultivating such steadiness, we can listen attentively without being distracted by personal biases or emotions. Listening with a calm, steady heart reflects this inner equipoise. We become instruments of peace in our relationships, channels through which understanding and love can flow.

Relevance

When we listen fully, we honor the other person's essence and cultivate deeper understanding, which is essential in building a strong, compassionate relationship. Listening with presence, as Krishna does with Arjuna, creates space for true communication, fostering mutual respect and spiritual connection.

Such listening transforms ordinary conversation into spiritual practice, where two souls meet in truth, patience, and divine connection. Listening, then, is not merely an act of communication—it is **satsanga**, a sacred communion that nourishes the heart and uplifts the soul.

Closing Thought

Just as Sita's quiet presence comforted Raj more than any words could, your gentle, attentive listening can become a source of healing and strength for someone today.

The more we practice this sacred art, the more we realize that true listening is an offering—a form of love that needs no reward, no validation. It simply opens the heart, allowing divine grace to flow between souls.

Four

Day 3: Recognizing Sacred Expressions of Love

Theme

Observe how your loved ones express love and identify their preferred sacred expression — Satya (Truthful Speech), Seva (Selfless Service), Sangha (Sacred Presence), Sparsha (Respectful Connection), or Dāna (Heartful Offering).

Story: A Day of Understanding Love

The morning sun peeked through the curtains as Sita sipped her tea, letting the warmth fill her senses. It was a peaceful start to the day, and she decided to pay close attention to how the people around her expressed love. Recently, she had been reflecting on the Bhagavad Gita's five sacred expressions of love—truthful speech, selfless service, sacred presence, respectful connection, and heartful offering.

Today, she wanted to observe how her loved ones naturally shared these divine expressions in their daily lives.

Morning: A Quiet Moment with Her Mother — Seva (Selfless Service)

As Sita helped her mother with breakfast, she noticed how her mom was always thoughtful about the small things—making her favorite tea just the right temperature and bringing her toast perfectly crisp.

"Here you go, dear," her mom said, placing the plate in front of her. "Just the way you like it."

Sita smiled softly. It was such a simple act, yet it spoke volumes about her mother's selfless love.

She realized that her mother's care reflected Seva, the sacred expression of love through humble service, offered without expectation of recognition.

> *"By performing one's duties without attachment, one attains the Supreme." — Bhagavad Gita 3.19*

Her mother's quiet service was a daily form of worship.

Afternoon: A Thoughtful Gesture from Her Friend — Dāna (Heartful Offering)

Later that day, Sita met her best friend, Seema, for lunch. As they caught up, Seema pulled out a small, wrapped box from her bag.

"I saw this and thought of you," she said with a grin.

Inside was a delicate silver bracelet—the same one Sita had admired weeks ago.

Touched by the thoughtfulness, Sita realized that this wasn't just about a gift. It was Dāna, the expression of love through a heartful offering, given with pure affection and remembrance.

> *"Whatever you give, whatever you offer, whatever you do—do it as an offering unto Me." — Bhagavad Gita 9.27*

Seema's gesture wasn't material—it was spiritual, born from love and remembrance.

Evening: A Moment of Comfort with Her Partner — Sparsha (Respectful Connection)

That evening, Sita and her husband Raj decided to unwind with a movie. As they settled on the couch, Raj gently took her hand, his thumb brushing lightly across her knuckles.

In that simple touch, Sita felt comfort, safety, and warmth. It wasn't just physical affection—it was Sparsha, the sacred touch that communicates reassurance and unity of hearts.

When Raj paused the movie to fetch her a blanket, she noticed another layer of love—Seva again, expressed through care and attentiveness.

> *"He who sees the Lord in all beings, and all beings in the Lord, never loses sight of Me." — Bhagavad Gita 6.30*

Through every touch and gesture, Raj reflected that divine unity.

Night: A Call from Her Father – Satya (Truthful Speech)

Just before bed, Sita received a call from her father. He had no particular reason to call—only to remind her how proud he was of her.

"I know you've been working hard, and I just want to say that I'm really proud of you, Sita," he said warmly.

Sita's heart swelled. His words, simple yet sincere, reflected Satya—truthful and uplifting speech. His encouragement always lifted her spirit, filling her with quiet strength and faith.

> *"Austerity of speech consists in speaking words that are truthful, pleasing, beneficial, and not agitating to others." — Bhagavad Gita 17.15*

Her father's voice was a reminder that truthful words have the power to heal and uplift.

Before Bed: A Cozy Conversation with Her Sister — Sangha (Sacred Presence)

Later that night, Sita sat with her younger sister, Urmila. They laughed, shared stories, and simply enjoyed being together. There was no agenda—only presence.

Sita realized that Urmila's way of expressing love was Sangha—the sacred act of being fully present. Their time together nourished her heart more deeply than words could express.

> *"One who is equal to friends and enemies, equipoised in honor and dishonor, is dear to Me." — Bhagavad Gita 12.18–19*

Sangha reflects this divine equality—showing up fully, with peace, acceptance, and presence.

Reflection

That night, as Sita lay in bed, she felt a profound gratitude for the many ways love flowed through her life. She thought of:

- Her mother's Seva – selfless acts of care.
- Seema's Dāna – a thoughtful, loving offering.
- Raj's Sparsha – the comfort of touch and care.
- Her father's Satya – kind and encouraging words.
- Urmila's Sangha – her warm, undistracted presence.

Each one reflected divine love in a unique way. Sita realized that recognizing these sacred expressions made her more aware of the divine essence in each person and deepened her appreciation for them.

Sita felt deeply grateful for the people in her life, and as she reflected on their unique ways of expressing love, she felt a renewed sense of connection and appreciation. Understanding their love expressions made her appreciate them even more, and she decided to make an effort to express her own love in ways that resonated with each of them.

Like Sita, we all express love in different ways. The key is to notice these gestures, no matter how small, and understand that they are a reflection of how others care for us. Recognizing these expressions of love can deepen our connections, fostering greater empathy and understanding, and making us more appreciative of the people we love.

Activity

Observe:

Throughout the day, notice how the people around you express love—through words, actions, presence, service, or gifts.

Reflect:

Which sacred expression—Satya, Seva, Sangha, Sparsha, or Dāna—best describes each person's way of loving?

Respond Consciously:

Try expressing love in their way. For example, if someone values Sangha, give them your full presence; if they express Seva, offer help without being asked.

Why Recognizing Sacred Expressions Matters

The Bhagavad Gita teaches that love is not confined to one form—it flows through every action, word, and intention. When we recognize and honor the unique ways others express their love, we cultivate understanding, empathy, and spiritual harmony.

This awareness transforms relationships from being transactional to transcendental, where every interaction becomes an offering to the Divine within each being.

> *"He who performs all actions as an offering to the Divine, without attachment, remains untouched by sin—just as a lotus leaf is untouched by water." — Bhagavad Gita 5.10*

When we love selflessly and with awareness, every moment becomes sacred.

Guided by the Bhagavad Gita

The Bhagavad Gita teaches that each individual has their unique dharma (purpose) and nature. By understanding how your loved ones express love, you honor their inherent qualities and spiritual path.

> *"It is better to perform one's own duty imperfectly than to perform another's duty perfectly. Better is death in one's own duty; the duty of another is fraught with fear." — Bhagavad Gita 3.35*

This verse emphasizes the importance of respecting each person's natural inclinations and actions. Just as Krishna encourages Arjuna to follow his own dharma, recognizing the unique ways your loved ones express love acknowledges their authentic path and honors their divine individuality.

Relevant Verses and Expressions

Satya (Truthful Speech):

"Speech that is truthful, pleasing, beneficial, and not agitating to others, and also the practice of yoga are dear to Me." — Bhagavad Gita 17.15

This highlights the importance of speaking with honesty, gentleness, and purpose—expressing love through words that uplift and bring peace.

Seva (Selfless Service):

"In the beginning, the Creator, having created mankind together with sacrifices, said: 'By this shall you prosper; let this be the milker of your desires.'" — Bhagavad Gita 3.10

Selfless service, performed as an offering to the Divine, sustains harmony and strengthens relationships through care and contribution without expectation.

Sangha (Sacred Presence):

"Let a man lift himself by his own self alone; let him not lower himself. For he alone is his own friend, and he alone is his own enemy." — Bhagavad Gita 6.5

Sacred presence is cultivated through mindfulness and inner balance. When we are present and centered, our company itself becomes a source of peace and upliftment to others.

Sparsha (Respectful Connection):

"He who sees Me in all beings, and all beings in Me, is never separated from Me, nor am I ever separated from him." — Bhagavad Gita 6.30

This verse reveals the divine unity underlying all relationships. Seeing the Divine within every person allows us to connect with respect, empathy, and unconditional love.

Dāna (Heartful Offering):

"That gift which is given out of duty, at the proper time and place, to a worthy person, and without expectation of return, is considered to be charity in the mode of goodness." — Bhagavad Gita 17.20

Dāna represents the love expressed through giving freely and joyfully—whether through time, attention, or support—without any expectation of reward.

Relevance

Observing and honoring these sacred expressions of love helps us cultivate understanding, empathy, and compassion. By aligning with the principles of the Bhagavad Gita, we learn that every act of love—whether through words, service, presence, connection, or offering—is a reflection of the Divine essence within each being.

Recognizing this sacred truth transforms relationships into spiritual partnerships, nurturing peace, harmony, and deeper soul connection in every interaction.

Closing Thought

Sita discovered that love isn't always spoken in grand declarations—it often shines through small, everyday gestures. When we learn to see these sacred expressions of love in others, we awaken to the divine flow that connects every heart.

By honoring these unique ways of loving, we create relationships rooted in understanding, grace, and devotion—making every act an offering of love to the Divine.

Five

Day 4: Being Fully Present

Theme

Spend quality time by giving your undivided attention to a loved one, free from distractions.

Story: A Quiet Moment with Mom

It was a sunny Saturday afternoon, and Avantika had been feeling the weight of her busy school week. Her mind was occupied with homework, her favorite books, and the excitement of an upcoming school event. Meanwhile, her mother was preparing snacks in the kitchen, humming softly to herself.

Avantika walked in, still lost in her thoughts, holding her favorite storybook. Her mother noticed and smiled warmly.

"Avantika, why don't you sit with me for a moment? Just you and me, no distractions. We'll have a cup of warm milk together."

Avantika hesitated but then put her book down and sat beside her mother. For the next fifteen minutes, they simply enjoyed each other's company. Avantika listened as her mother shared the little joys of her day—how the garden had bloomed with the recent rains and how she was planning a new recipe for dinner. It wasn't the most exciting conversation, but it was filled with warmth and attention.

As her mother spoke, Avantika realized how often she was caught up in her own thoughts, even in the presence of those she cared about. But now, giving her full attention to her mother, she felt a deeper sense of connection. The small moments—those that seemed insignificant at first—were actually where the true bond was built.

"Avantika, I'm so glad we could do this," her mother said after a while, smiling. "It's the simple things that matter."

Avantika nodded, grateful. "Me too, Mom. I'm glad I listened."

Reflection

Like Avantika, we often overlook the importance of giving someone our full attention. In today's world, distractions are everywhere. Yet, when we choose to be present, giving someone our undivided focus, we not only deepen the emotional connection but also make the other person feel truly seen, valued, and heard.

The Bhagavad Gita reminds us that presence is a form of devotion—an act of mindfulness and self-mastery. When the mind is steady and focused, the heart naturally becomes more open and compassionate.

Activity

1. Reflect:

- Take a moment to think about how often you give your loved ones your full attention.
- Are you easily distracted by your phone, TV, or other devices when spending time with them?
- What effect do you think this has on your relationships?

2. Undivided Attention:

- Choose a loved one—whether it's a parent, partner, child, or friend—and spend 10–15 minutes today with no distractions.
- Put your phone away, turn off notifications, and focus entirely on them.
- Listen actively, maintain eye contact, and engage with genuine interest in what they're saying.

Why Being Present Matters

Being fully present in the moment is one of the most sacred ways to express love and honor another soul. By giving someone your complete attention, you reflect the qualities of Sankalpa (intentional awareness) and Samatvam (inner balance) as taught in the Gita.

Distractions pull the mind outward, but presence brings it inward—to the heart. When you listen deeply and respond with care, you create harmony, trust, and emotional safety. This attentive awareness mirrors the calm and centered mind of a yogi—anchored in the present, undisturbed by external fluctuations.

Guided by the Bhagavad Gita

The Bhagavad Gita emphasizes the importance of being anchored in the present moment. By being fully attentive, we reflect inner peace, mindfulness, and self-awareness, fostering deeper connection and authenticity in our relationships.

Relevant Verses:

- **Chapter 5, Verse 11:**
- "The wise, acting with body, mind, intellect, and senses, without attachment, only for the purification of the self, remain ever content."

This verse teaches that mindful action, performed with awareness and detachment, purifies the heart and brings inner peace.

- **Chapter 6, Verse 25:**
- "Gradually, step by step, with determination, one should become situated in trance by means of intelligence, and thus the mind should be fixed on the Self alone, thinking of nothing else."

This verse highlights patience and focus—the foundations of presence and mindfulness.

Being present with a loved one reflects this state of inner steadiness and divine attention. It is not about doing more but about being more—aware, connected, and compassionate in the moment.

Relevance

When we give our undivided attention, we offer the most precious gift—the gift of presence. It strengthens emotional bonds and fosters trust, understanding, and intimacy.

In those quiet moments of connection, we live the essence of the Gita: acting with awareness, rooted in balance, and free from distraction or attachment.

Closing Thought

As Avantika realized, sometimes it's the smallest, most ordinary moments—free from distraction—that carry the deepest love.

When we give our loved ones our full attention, we mirror the divine quality of Samatvam—equanimity of the heart—and remind them that they are truly cherished and significant in our lives.

To be present is to love completely, just as the Gita teaches—to act with mindfulness, steadiness, and a heart anchored in peace.

Six

Day 5: Empathy Check-In

Theme

Reflect on a loved one's recent challenges and take a moment to consider their feelings and needs with compassion and discernment.

Story: The Silent Support

It had been a long week for Sita. Her work had been overwhelming, and she felt like she was carrying the weight of the world on her shoulders. Despite her best efforts, there were days when she felt emotionally drained, but she kept it to herself, not wanting to burden anyone.

One evening, her partner, Raj, sat beside her on the couch, sensing something was off. Without saying a word, he handed her a cup of tea and settled next to her quietly, wrapping a blanket around her shoulders.

"I noticed you've been a little distant lately," Raj said gently, his voice full of concern. "Is there anything you want to talk about, or do you just need some time to relax?"

Sita blinked, taken aback by his sensitivity. She hadn't realized how much she had needed someone to notice her emotions, to see beyond the façade. She had been so absorbed in her responsibilities that she hadn't taken a moment to acknowledge or process her feelings.

"I think I just need to rest," Sita murmured. "But thank you for noticing. It means more to me than you know."

Raj smiled softly and gave her a reassuring squeeze.

"I'm here, always. No need to explain."

That evening, Sita took the time to sit with her feelings, grateful for Raj's quiet presence and empathetic support. It was a small gesture, but one that made her feel deeply understood and cared for.

Later, she texted him:

"Thank you for being there for me tonight. I didn't realize how much I needed your support. It means everything to me."

Raj replied,

"I'm always here to listen, love. Just let me know when you're ready to talk."

Reflection

Like Sita, we often carry emotional burdens without realizing how much we long to be seen, understood, and supported. Empathy, or Karunā, is not about fixing another's problems—it is about opening the heart to feel what the other feels and standing beside them with silent strength and presence.

The Bhagavad Gita teaches that a wise person, guided by Viveka (discernment), acts not out of impulse or judgment but from understanding and compassion. True empathy is born from this balance—the heart's softness guided by the mind's clarity.

To practice Karunā is to see the divine essence within the other person—to recognize that their joys and sorrows are reflections of the same universal soul that resides in all.

Activity

1. Reflect:

Think about someone in your life who may be going through a difficult time. What challenges might they be facing? How might they be feeling within? Take a moment to contemplate their emotional state without judgment—only with gentle awareness.

2. Empathy in Action:

Reach out to that person with a heart of compassion. You don't need to offer solutions—simply offer your presence.

You might say:

> *"I've been thinking of you and wanted to check in. How are you feeling today? I'm here if you'd like to share."*

Let your words arise from sincerity and stillness, reflecting the Gita's teaching of selfless care—helping not to change, but to comfort.

Why Empathy Matters

Empathy bridges hearts. When we take time to understand another's inner experience, we dissolve separation and create unity. The Gita reminds us that the enlightened soul sees all beings with equality—in joy and sorrow alike.

Through empathy, we align with divine consciousness, recognizing that love is not only expressed in action but in awareness. By simply being present and open, we allow healing energy to flow naturally.

True empathy requires both Karunā (compassion) and Viveka (discernment)—compassion to feel another's pain, and discernment to remain steady, not consumed by it. Together, they form the spiritual foundation for emotional maturity and deep connection.

Guided by the Bhagavad Gita

The Bhagavad Gita emphasizes seeing the divine essence in all beings. By practicing empathy, we acknowledge the inherent divinity in others, understanding their challenges and responding with care and compassion.

Relevant Verse:

- **Chapter 5, Verse 18:**
- "The humble sage, by virtue of true knowledge, sees with equal vision a learned and gentle brāhmaṇa, a cow, an elephant, a dog, and a dog-eater."

This verse teaches that recognizing the divine essence in all beings allows us to respond with compassion, transcending judgment or prejudice.

- **Chapter 6, Verse 32:**
- "He who sees the happiness and distress of others as his own is considered the highest yogi."

Krishna describes this as the ultimate form of connection—where compassion and oneness merge.

- **Chapter 12, Verses 13-14:**
- "He who is free from malice toward all beings, friendly and compassionate, without attachment and ego, balanced in happiness and distress, and forgiving—such a devotee is very dear to Me."

These verses define the spirit of Karunā: gentle understanding, forgiveness, and emotional balance.

Relevance

Empathy, when practiced as the Gita teaches, becomes a sacred act—an offering from the soul.

It is the awareness that beneath all emotions, struggles, and masks lies the same divine spark. When we approach others with this realization, our relationships transform into spiritual connections founded on trust, understanding, and unconditional love.

Closing Thought

Like Raj's quiet gesture, true empathy needs no grand expression—it shines in silence, in presence, in understanding without words.

To practice Karunā with Viveka is to embody the wisdom of the Gita: to feel deeply yet remain inwardly balanced, to love purely without expectation.

When we meet others with such compassion, we not only comfort their hearts—we awaken the divine within our own.

> *"He who sees Me in all beings, and all beings in Me, never loses sight of Me."*

— Bhagavad Gita 6.30

Seven

Day 6: Acts of Selfless Love

Theme

Show love to a loved one through selfless action, without expecting anything in return.

Story: A Gesture of Love

Sita walked into the kitchen, her mind busy with the tasks of the day. She had been running errands all afternoon, trying to keep up with her endless list. But as she entered the room, she noticed something unusual—her husband, Raj, was at the stove, carefully chopping vegetables for dinner.

"I thought you could use some help tonight," Raj said with a smile, turning to her as she walked in. "You've been working hard all week, and I just wanted to make things easier for you."

Sita's heart softened at the sight. Raj knew her sacred way of receiving love—Seva (selfless service)—and though they never explicitly discussed it, he always seemed to sense when she was running low on energy and needed a hand. His thoughtful gesture spoke louder than words. The small act, offered without any expectation, was an expression of Nishkama Karma—selfless action performed with love.

Later that evening, after dinner, their daughter Avantika walked in holding a handmade card.

"Mom, I made this for you," she said, handing Sita the colorful card. On it were drawings of flowers and hearts, and a simple message that read, "I love you, Mom."

Sita smiled warmly at Avantika. "Thank you, sweetheart," she said, hugging her daughter. "This means so much to me."

Raj, seeing this exchange, turned to Avantika and gently placed his hand on her shoulder.

"You know, sweetheart," he said, "sometimes the best way to show love is in the little things—whether it's helping with something, giving a hug, or creating something with your heart. Love isn't about reward—it's about giving with sincerity."

Avantika beamed. "I love drawing for you, Mom! And I love when you cook my favorite food, Dad," she said, looking at both of them with affection.

Sita paused, realizing how her family expressed love in different ways—Raj through service, Avantika through heartfelt offerings, and herself through quality time and warmth. Each of them was expressing love in their own sacred form, and together, it created a beautiful harmony in their home.

Reflection

Small, thoughtful gestures can often mean the most. Raj, Avantika, and Sita each expressed love in ways that reflected the Bhagavad Gita's sacred expressions of love.

- Raj expressed his love through **Seva** — selfless service, performing his duties with care and devotion, without expecting anything in return.
- Avantika expressed her love through **Dāna** — heartfelt offering, sharing her handmade gift with affection and sincerity.
- Sita expressed her love through **Sangha** and **Sparsha** — quality time and gentle connection that nurtured warmth and presence within the family.

These simple, heartfelt acts deepened their emotional connection, proving that love isn't about what we receive, but about giving from the heart. Each gesture, no matter how small, became a reflection of the Bhagavad Gita's timeless teachings on love as Seva (selfless action), Dāna (generosity), Sangha (presence), and Sparsha (compassionate connection)—transforming everyday moments into sacred offerings of the heart.

Activity

1. Reflect:

Think about someone close to you—whether a partner, friend, or family member. How can you serve them with love, without expecting anything in return?

2. Express Seva:

Perform a small, thoughtful act of kindness for them today. It may be helping with a task, preparing a meal, giving your full attention, offering words of appreciation, or simply being present with them.

Why Small Acts of Kindness Matter

According to the Bhagavad Gita, every action becomes sacred when performed without selfish desire. When we act with a spirit of offering—without attachment to results—our hearts become pure, and relationships naturally grow in harmony.

These small acts of Seva, done with love and mindfulness, carry transformative power. They shift the energy of relationships, dissolve ego, and create an atmosphere of mutual respect, care, and divine connection.

Guided by the Bhagavad Gita

The Bhagavad Gita emphasizes performing actions selflessly, without attachment to outcomes. Small acts of kindness, given with genuine intention and without expectation of return, reflect the essence of selfless love (**Nishkama Karma**) and contribute to the well-being of others.

Relevant Verse:

- ***Chapter 3, Verse 19:***
- "Therefore, without being attached to the fruits of activities, one should act as a matter of duty, for by working without attachment, one attains the Supreme." (BG 3.19)

This verse reminds us that love and service, when offered without attachment to outcome, become spiritual practices. Each act of kindness becomes a form of **Seva**—a humble offering to the Divine within others.

Relevance

Selfless actions performed with a pure heart deepen the bond between individuals. They are not just gestures—they are offerings of love that harmonize relationships and nurture the soul.

When kindness flows freely, without the expectation of return, it becomes a reflection of divine love—transforming ordinary moments into sacred ones.

Closing Thought

Like Raj's quiet gesture, Avantika's heartfelt card, and Sita's nurturing love, your small acts of kindness can become powerful expressions of devotion. When love is expressed through selfless action, it nourishes the hearts of all involved and creates a ripple of peace and joy that extends far beyond the moment.

Try it today—offer a small act of kindness with love, and witness how it uplifts both you and those around you.

Eight

Day 7: The Power of Self-Reflection

Theme

Reflect on how your actions made you feel and any changes you noticed in your connections.

Story: A Week of Small Changes

A soft evening breeze fluttered the curtains in Sita's living room as she sat with her journal, a warm cup of tea in hand. It had been a week of small, intentional actions—expressing gratitude, offering kindness, and practicing mindful presence with her loved ones. She had been focused on strengthening bonds, but now, as the week came to a close, it was time to reflect on how those actions had made her feel.

Her daughter, Avantika, was finishing up her homework in the corner of the room when Sita decided to start her self-reflection.

"Avantika, remember how we spent some quality time together yesterday?" Sita asked gently, setting the journal aside.

Avantika looked up from her notebook and smiled.

"Yes, Mom! We read that story about the bird who didn't give up. It was fun."

Sita nodded, her heart warmed by the memory.

"Do you think that time we spent together made a difference?" she asked.

Avantika thought for a moment, then shrugged happily.

"I think so. I liked it. We don't always do that, but it was nice."

Sita smiled and reflected on her own feelings. She had noticed that when she gave Avantika her undivided attention—no distractions, just the two of them—she felt a stronger connection to her daughter. That time had allowed her to appreciate the small moments that often went unnoticed in their busy lives. It had felt good to be present, to focus on nothing else but the relationship they were nurturing.

Later that evening, as Sita sat down with her husband, Raj, she asked softly,

"How did it feel when I took the time to express my gratitude for all the little things you do around the house?"

Her voice carried warmth, seeking not just an answer, but a deeper connection.

Raj looked up from his book and smiled.

"Honestly? It felt great. I didn't expect it, but hearing that you noticed made me feel appreciated. I think it even made me want to do more for us."

Sita realized that Raj's response showed how simple **Satya** (Truthful & Uplifting Speech) could have a profound effect on their relationship. In those few moments of genuine appreciation, she had strengthened their bond without even realizing it.

Reflecting on these small actions brought clarity to Sita's mind. She realized that kindness, mindful attention, and gratitude weren't just things to do for others—they also brought her a deeper sense of inner peace and fulfillment. She had noticed subtle changes: she felt more connected to Avantika, and Raj seemed more engaged and joyful after she expressed her appreciation. Even though these were small gestures, they had a big impact.

As she wrote in her journal that evening, Sita acknowledged the importance of self-reflection (**Svadhyaya**). It was a simple yet powerful tool to measure the impact of her efforts in building stronger, more meaningful connections.

Reflection

Self-reflection had opened her eyes to the beautiful, quiet growth that had already unfolded in her relationships. It was not just the gestures but the way her heart had shifted towards more love, understanding, and inner steadiness (**Sthitaprajna**).

She noticed that her connection with Avantika deepened when they spent uninterrupted time together, and Raj seemed happier when she expressed gratitude. These were positive shifts, and they made her realize the importance of being intentional about her actions.

Activity:

Reflect

Take a moment to think about the small acts of kindness, attention, or expressions of gratitude you shared over the past week.

- How did those moments make you feel—both in the giving and

the receiving?
- What changes have you noticed in your relationships?

Examples for Reflection:

- **For Parents (from a child's perspective):**
- "When I helped Mom with chores, I felt proud. I noticed she was grateful, and it made me feel more connected to her."
- **For Life Partner (from your perspective):**
- "When I thanked my partner for their support, I noticed they seemed happier and more open to spending time with me."
- **For a Friend (from your perspective):**
- "Sending my friend a note of appreciation helped me feel closer to them. I realized how important it is to express gratitude for the people I care about."
- **For a Child (from a parent's perspective):**
- "Spending quality time with Avantika reminded me how much she needs my undivided attention. It felt good to give her my full focus."

Why Self-Reflection Matters

Self-reflection allows you to understand the true impact of your actions, not just on your relationships, but on your own heart. It shows you the subtle shifts of connection that often go unnoticed, helping you nurture deeper bonds with those who matter most.

It allows you to identify positive changes and acknowledge the growth in your connections. By understanding how showing kindness, expressing gratitude, or being fully present made you feel, you strengthen emotional bonds and cultivate inner stability.

This practice deepens your awareness of how your choices contribute to the health, harmony, and happiness of your relationships.

Reminder

- Take a moment to pause and reflect on your actions.
- Even if things didn't go perfectly, be kind to yourself.
- Every step you take toward improving your relationships is progress.

Use reflection as an opportunity to learn, grow, and continue building deeper, loving connections.

Tip

- When reflecting, celebrate small victories.
- Even small, intentional actions like offering a compliment, giving undivided attention, or expressing gratitude can create meaningful changes in your relationships.

Guided by the Bhagavad Gita

Self-reflection, or **Svadhyaya**, is at the heart of the Gita's teachings. By examining our thoughts, words, and actions, we cultivate self-awareness and inner stability (**Sthitaprajna**), which supports deeper connections with others and ourselves.

Relevant Verse:

- **Chapter 6, Verse 5** – Krishna reminds us that true spiritual progress begins with self-awareness:

"Let a man lift himself by his own self alone; let him not lower

himself. For he alone is his own friend, and he alone is his own enemy."

This verse teaches that true spiritual progress begins with self-awareness. Through introspection, we understand our tendencies, motivations, and the effects of our actions on others, fostering conscious and compassionate living.

Relevance

- Self-reflection is vital for personal growth and understanding how our behavior affects our relationships.
- Through introspection, we become more conscious of our patterns and can make mindful choices to foster healthier and more harmonious relationships.
- By practicing **Svadhyaya** and cultivating **Sthitaprajna**, we strengthen our inner foundation, allowing love, compassion, and presence to naturally flow in all connections.

Closing Thought

Reflecting on our actions is not just a tool for growth—it is a way to deepen our connections, heal what needs healing, and cultivate relationships filled with understanding, compassion, and steadiness.

By understanding how our efforts, no matter how small, contribute to stronger connections, we can continue nurturing and building our bonds with others.

It's through these reflections that we learn, evolve, and create lasting, meaningful connections rooted in love and inner peace.

Nine

Day 8: Expressing Appreciation

Theme

Tell someone you care about one specific thing you truly admire about them.

Story: A Heartfelt Compliment

The evening was settling in, wrapping the home in a cozy warmth. In the quiet of the kitchen, Sita sat at the kitchen table, watching her mother Lalitha prepare dinner. The aroma of spices filled the air, and the rhythmic chop of vegetables echoed through the room. Sita had always admired her mother's cooking, but today, as she watched her mother's graceful movements and the care with which she prepared each dish, something about it felt even more intimate and profound.

"You know, Mom," Sita said softly, breaking the silence, "I really admire how you cook. Every meal you make is always so full of love. It's like you've turned cooking into an art form."

Lalitha looked up from the stove, her face lighting up with a gentle smile.

"Thank you, beta," she said, her voice full of warmth. "I just want to make sure everyone feels at home."

Sita's heart swelled with affection as she realized how often she overlooked her mother's quiet acts of care. It wasn't just the meals, but the love and intention that went into every little thing she did for the family. Sita was grateful for the chance to express her appreciation.

Later, when they sat down to eat together, there was an extra layer of warmth and connection in the room—a feeling that had been deepened by a simple, heartfelt compliment. It was a small but meaningful moment that would stay with them both.

Reflection

Much like Sita, we sometimes forget to express appreciation for the people who matter most. When we take the time to acknowledge the unique qualities or actions of those we love, we create a deeper emotional connection.

A simple compliment, when given sincerely, reflects **Kritajñatā** (gratitude) and **Satya** (truthfulness). It allows both the giver and receiver to feel seen, valued, and understood, fostering harmony and goodwill in relationships.

Activity: How to Express Appreciation

Reflect:

Think about someone close to you—a parent, partner, friend, or child. Reflect on a specific, meaningful quality or action they've shown recently that has touched your heart or made a difference in your life.

Examples of Expressing Appreciation:

- **For Parents:**
- "Mom, I admire how you make every meal feel like a celebration. Your care and thoughtfulness really stand out."
- **For Life Partner:**
- "I appreciate how patient you are with me when I'm feeling overwhelmed. Your calmness helps me feel grounded."
- **For a Friend:**
- "I admire your ability to always listen without judgment. Your support means the world to me."
- **For a Child:**
- "I love how imaginative you are when you draw. Your creativity brightens my day."

Express Appreciation:

Once you've identified what you admire, express it in a way that feels right—whether through a phone call, handwritten note, or heartfelt conversation. Be specific about the quality or action you're acknowledging.

Why Appreciation Matters

When we express appreciation, we honor the unique qualities and efforts of others. Genuine words of acknowledgment, rooted in truth and kindness, nurture respect, trust, and deeper emotional bonds.

This practice strengthens relationships and fosters a positive, uplifting environment. By appreciating others without expectation, we cultivate harmony, gratitude, and love—principles deeply embedded in the Bhagavad Gita.

Guided by the Bhagavad Gita

The Bhagavad Gita teaches that speech should be truthful, kind, and beneficial, forming the foundation of sincere communication and connection. By expressing appreciation with authenticity and devotion, we honor the divine essence in others and cultivate harmonious relationships.

Relevant Verses:

- **Chapter 17, Verse 14 – Austerity of Speech:**
- "The austerity of speech consists in speaking words that are truthful, pleasing, and beneficial; words that do not cause distress to others, and words that are in accordance with dharma and spiritual discipline."
- **Chapter 17, Verse 15 – Austerity of Eating:**
- "The austerity of eating consists of consuming food that is pure, wholesome, and agreeable, which sustains life, strength, health, happiness, and satisfaction. Eating in moderation, without overindulgence, is part of this discipline."
- **Chapter 17, Verse 16 – Austerity of Work and Recreation:**
- "The austerity of work and recreation consists in engaging in

activities with self-discipline, without attachment or disturbance to others, and in a way that maintains balance, cleanliness, and devotion. Work and enjoyment done in this manner purify the mind and heart."

These verses emphasize that words, actions, and even recreation, when practiced with discipline, devotion, and truth, lead to purification and foster trust, understanding, and love in relationships. Expressing genuine appreciation aligns with this teaching. Speaking with truth (**Satya**), kindness, and sincerity fosters goodwill, strengthens relationships, and nurtures emotional bonds.

Relevance

- Verbal appreciation enhances emotional bonds and reflects the Bhagavad Gita's principles of truth and kindness.
- Acknowledging others without expectation nurtures respect, deepens trust, and leads to stronger, more meaningful connections.

Closing Thought

A compliment, though small, can spark a ripple effect of warmth, love, and connection. Just as Sita's words brought a smile to her mother's face, your words of admiration and gratitude can uplift spirits and bring people closer together.

By continuing to recognize and share the qualities you admire, you contribute to a more positive, nurturing, and fulfilling environment for both yourself and those around you.

Ten

Day 9: Observing Without Judgment

Theme

Practice awareness of others' words and actions without labeling, judging, or reacting impulsively.

Story: The Quiet Garden

It was a warm afternoon, and Sita sat under the shade of their old neem tree, her legs crossed beneath her, sipping a cup of tea as she watched Raj carefully tend to the flowers. His hands were steady, moving methodically as he pruned the roses and trimmed the hedges. The soft hum of the garden seemed to slow everything down, but Sita's mind was elsewhere.

All morning, she had been rushing from one chore to the next, trying to keep up with the laundry, the dishes, and the bills. She looked over at Raj again. He had been out there for hours, absorbed in the peaceful rhythm of gardening, and a quiet stirring rose within her—a mix of admiration and frustration, but mostly a longing for peace of her own.

Why doesn't he see that I'm drowning in tasks? she thought, feeling the familiar weight of resentment rise. He was lost in his own world, and she couldn't help but feel frustrated.

But as she sat there, her frustration slowly simmered down. She took a deep breath and let it out slowly, deciding to try something different. Instead of labeling his actions as "careless" or "thoughtless," she simply watched him. She noticed the way his fingers delicately moved between the leaves, how he took his time with each plant, ensuring it was well cared for. His focus was complete, almost meditative. She realized, for the first time, that gardening wasn't just a hobby for Raj—it was his way of grounding himself, a way of finding peace.

Sita's heart softened. She could see the care and attention he gave to every plant, and she remembered how he'd always been the one to manage the garden, pouring his love into it season after season. It wasn't that he didn't care for her or the home; he just expressed his love differently. His act of tending to the garden was as much about his need for peace as it was about nurturing something beautiful.

When Raj came inside later that evening, the cool evening air wrapped around them, and the scent of freshly cut flowers lingered in the room. Sita looked up from the stove, where she was finishing dinner.

"I noticed how much time you spent with the garden today," she said, her voice soft. "It's really beautiful, how much care you put into it. I can tell it means a lot to you."

Raj paused for a moment, surprised by the warmth in her words. He smiled, his tired eyes lighting up with gratitude.

"Thanks, Sita. It helps me unwind after a busy week."

Sita hesitated but then decided to speak up about how she'd been feeling earlier. She didn't want to accuse him or put him on the defensive.

"I've been feeling a bit overwhelmed today," she admitted. "I guess I didn't express it well, but I could really use some help around the house. Sometimes I assume you know what I need, but I realize I haven't been clear about it."

Raj listened quietly, his expression open. He didn't feel attacked or blamed; instead, he felt a sense of clarity.

"I get it," he said, giving her a reassuring smile. "I'll try to be more aware of that next time. Let me know how I can help."

Together, they found a way to balance both their needs, laughing as they agreed to share the tasks in a way that worked for both of them. It felt good to speak openly, without assumptions or judgments, and it deepened their connection, creating a more peaceful understanding between them.

Reflection

Just like Sita, we can sometimes misinterpret others' actions through the lens of our expectations and judgments. By observing without labeling behaviors as "good" or "bad," we allow ourselves to see the situation with clarity and balance.

This practice reflects **Sthitaprajna** (equanimity) and **Samatvam** (even-mindedness), allowing us to respond with understanding rather than reaction. Observing without judgment creates space for compassion, helping us nurture more harmonious and peaceful relationships.

Activity

Reflect:

Think about a recent situation where you may have judged someone's actions—whether it was a family member, friend, or colleague.

- How did you label their behavior?
- What assumptions did you make about their intentions?
- How might your perspective have shifted if you had simply observed the situation without judgment, allowing for a clearer understanding of the other person's experience?

Observing Without Judgment:

As you go about your day, consciously practice observing someone's behavior without attaching any judgment.

- Notice what is happening without labeling it as "good" or "bad."
- For example, if you see someone on their phone while you're talking, simply observe: "They are looking at their phone."
- Resist the urge to label it as "disrespectful" or "thoughtless."

Why Observing Without Judgment Matters

By observing others without judgment, we respond with clarity, equanimity, and compassion. We see situations as they truly are—free from assumptions, biases, or emotional reactions.

This practice reflects the Bhagavad Gita's teaching of non-attachment and equanimity, fostering mindfulness and reducing conflicts. By detaching from judgment, we cultivate understanding, harmony, and deeper connection in our relationships.

Guided by the Bhagavad Gita

The Bhagavad Gita teaches us to rise above judgment and cultivate non-attachment, which includes detaching from preconceived notions or expectations of others. By observing without judgment, we create mental balance and foster compassionate understanding.

Relevant Verse:

- **Chapter 6, Verse 5:**
- "One must elevate, not degrade, oneself with one's own mind. The mind alone is the friend of the soul, and the mind alone is the enemy of the soul." (BG 6.5)

This verse emphasizes that the mind can either uplift or diminish us based on how it is trained. By cultivating awareness and letting go of judgments, we align with inner balance (**Sthitaprajna**) and develop equanimity (**Samatvam**), which allows us to interact with others without ego interference or bias.

Relevance

Observing without judgment allows us to communicate with clarity and without ego interference, creating an atmosphere of mutual respect. When we detach from judgment, we create space for compassion and empathy, helping to foster deeper understanding in relationships. Practicing this daily creates a foundation of mutual respect, harmony, and peaceful relationships.

Closing Thought

Observing without judgment isn't about ignoring our feelings—it's about creating the space to understand and communicate with others thoughtfully and compassionately.

By practicing **Sthitaprajna** and **Samatvam**, we bring more empathy, openness, and harmony into our relationships. This skill fosters peaceful conversations, mutual respect, and a balanced, loving connection with others.

Eleven

Day 10: Forgiveness and Letting Go

Theme

Identify a small hurt or disappointment and practice forgiveness and compassion to release negative emotions.

Story: A Moment of Understanding

It was a quiet Saturday afternoon when Avantika sat at the kitchen table, feeling a little disappointed. Her mother, Sita, had promised they would spend the afternoon baking her favorite cookies, but as the minutes ticked by, Sita was nowhere to be found.

Avantika had been looking forward to this special time, but instead, Sita had been busy with her own tasks, rushing around to get ready for the evening family gathering.

"Why is she always so busy?" Avantika thought, feeling a small pang of frustration. "She promised we'd spend time together, and now I'm here alone."

Sita had always been a loving and caring mother, but this small letdown made Avantika feel overlooked. It wasn't the first time something like this had happened, and Avantika found herself growing upset, replaying the disappointment in her mind.

As she walked past her mother in the living room, Sita noticed her daughter's downcast face.

"Hey, what's going on?" she asked, her tone soft and concerned.

"I was looking forward to baking with you today, but it seems like you've been busy with everything else," Avantika replied, trying to keep the sadness out of her voice.

Sita paused, guilt flashing across her face.

"Oh, sweetie, I didn't mean to let you down. I'm so sorry. I've just been caught up with some things, but that doesn't mean you're not important to me."

Avantika felt a wave of relief wash over her. Her mother wasn't ignoring her on purpose; she was just overwhelmed with responsibilities.

"I understand, Mom. I know you've got a lot on your plate," Avantika said, smiling a little. "I'll go ahead and start with the cookies while you finish up. We can do it together later."

Sita smiled warmly, walking over and wrapping her arms around Avantika.

"Thank you for being so understanding. I promise we'll get our baking session in soon."

And just like that, the small hurt faded away, replaced by the warmth of understanding and compassion.

Reflection

Like Avantika, we may experience small disappointments in our relationships, but it's in these moments that forgiveness can heal the emotional weight we carry.

Instead of letting the hurt fester, practicing **Kshamā** (forgiveness) frees us from resentment, allowing us to move forward with compassion, equanimity, and inner peace.

Forgiveness frees us from negative emotions, creating space for love and understanding to flourish.

Activity

Reflect

- Think about a small hurt or disappointment you've experienced recently.
- It could be a missed promise or a misunderstanding with a family member.
- How did it affect you emotionally, and what thoughts arose?

Forgiveness Practice

- Consciously release the negative emotions attached to this incident.
- Acknowledge that while the hurt is real, it need not define your emotions or choices.
- Let go of resentment and choose compassion, allowing space for healing and peace.

Why Forgiveness Matters

Forgiveness is not about excusing behavior but about choosing inner peace over frustration, reflecting **Kshamā** and **Nishkama Karma**. It creates space for emotional healing and the growth of compassion in our hearts.

By releasing negative emotions, we align with the Gita's teaching of non-attachment, allowing love and compassion to thrive in our relationships. Holding onto anger, resentment, or pain affects not only the mind but also the body, mood, and energy. Unforgiveness weighs us down like an emotional burden, blocking joy and inner peace.

Letting go lightens that load, making space for positivity, clarity, and inner harmony. Forgiveness also fosters stronger connections: by releasing resentment, we rebuild trust, deepen relationships, and allow love to flourish.

Most importantly, forgiveness is a gift to ourselves—a conscious choice to break free from emotional chains, embracing freedom, peace, and healing, just as Krishna teaches in the Bhagavad Gita.

Guided by the Bhagavad Gita

The Bhagavad Gita emphasizes forgiveness (**Kshamā**) as a divine quality essential for spiritual growth. By practicing forgiveness, we release anger and resentment, cultivate inner peace, and align with selfless action (**Nishkama Karma**). Letting go of past hurts allows us to interact with others from a place of love and equanimity, fostering harmony and emotional freedom in our relationships.

Relevant Verse:

- **Chapter 16, Verse 3:**

"Fearlessness, purity of heart, steadfastness in knowledge and yoga, charity, control of the senses, sacrifice, study of scriptures, austerity, and uprightness—these are the divine qualities." (BG 16.3)

This verse highlights that forgiveness (**Kshamā**) is among the divine qualities to cultivate. By embodying these qualities, we transform our hearts, letting go of attachment, resentment, or grudges, and create space for compassionate, selfless interaction.

Relevance

- Letting go of past hurts reflects the Gita's teachings of non-attachment and compassion.
- Forgiveness heals the heart and restores trust in relationships.
- Forgiveness liberates the self, paving the way for spiritual and emotional freedom.

Closing Thought

Just like Avantika chose to forgive and move forward, you too can let go of small hurts that hold you back.

Forgiveness is a powerful choice that aligns with selfless action and non-attachment, helping you release negativity and create space for healing and growth.

It allows love, understanding, and compassion to flourish, fostering deeper connection and trust in your relationships.

Twelve

Day 11: Understanding Needs Through Sacred Expressions of Love

Theme

Reflect on what makes you feel spiritually nourished and discuss it with a loved one to deepen mutual understanding.

Story: A Heartfelt Conversation

It was a peaceful evening when Sita and her family were gathered in the living room. Avantika was playing with her toys, Lalitha and Raghav were chatting softly in the corner, and Raj was leafing through a magazine. But something was on Sita's mind.

She had been thinking about how they all express love differently and how important it was to understand one another's needs.

"Sita, is everything okay?" Raj asked, noticing the thoughtful expression on her face.

"I've been reflecting on how we show care and nurture one another," Sita said. "Each of us has different ways of giving and receiving love. I want to understand what makes you feel spiritually nourished, and I want to share what nourishes me too."

"Expressions of love? What do you mean?" Raj asked with curiosity.

Sita explained, "Each person experiences care differently. Some of us feel nourished through selfless acts of service (**Seva**), some through mindful presence together (**Sangha**), others through sincere, uplifting words (**Satya**), meaningful offerings (**Dana**), or respectful, compassionate touch (**Sparsha**). Understanding each other's nature helps us serve and support one another in alignment with dharma."

Avantika, who had been quietly listening, looked up from her toys. "What makes me feel loved, Mama?" she asked curiously.

Sita smiled. "I think you truly enjoy hugs and closeness (**Sparsha**). You seem happiest when we share moments of affectionate presence."

Avantika beamed. "Yes! I love it when we hug!"

Raj chuckled. "I feel nourished when you do small, selfless things for me, like helping me or supporting tasks (**Seva**). That shows love."

Sita nodded, appreciating the insight. "For me, it's spending mindful time together (**Sangha**). I feel the most loved when we can simply be present with each other, talking or sitting quietly."

Lalitha, who had been listening, spoke up. "I feel nurtured when you all speak with kindness and truth (**Satya**). Even a simple heartfelt conversation or presence means the world."

Sita smiled warmly at her family. "See, we all express love differently, but once we understand each other's sacred expressions of love, we can honor one another's nature and deepen our connection."

Reflection

Like Sita's family, we may discover that our loved ones express love in different ways.

- Understanding each other's sacred expressions of love allows us to serve and connect in ways that resonate most deeply.
- It strengthens emotional bonds and fosters harmonious relationships.
- Recognizing how each person experiences care helps us honor their unique nature, promoting mutual respect and spiritual growth.

Activity

Reflect

- Think about what makes you feel nurtured and cared for.
- Do you feel most supported through selfless service (**Seva**), mindful presence (**Sangha**), sincere words (**Satya**), meaningful offerings (**Dana**), or compassionate touch (**Sparsha**)?
- Reflect on your own sacred expressions of love and how they shape your relationships.

Practice

- Share your needs and sacred expressions of love with someone close—partner, parent, or friend.
- Ask them to share theirs as well.
- Incorporate each other's needs into your interactions to strengthen connection and harmony.

Why Understanding Needs Matters

When we understand how each person gives and receives love, we honor their unique nature and can serve them meaningfully.

- Recognizing sacred expressions of love nurtures trust, empathy, and deeper connection.
- It helps us appreciate differences, fostering respect and compassion.
- Understanding needs allows us to build relationships that are both emotionally and spiritually fulfilling.

Guided by the Bhagavad Gita

The Bhagavad Gita encourages us to understand and honor the unique qualities and nature of each individual. Just as every person has a **Swadharma** (own nature or duty), they also have their own preferred way of expressing and receiving love—through **Satya** (truthful speech), **Seva** (selfless service), **Sangha** (sacred presence), **Sparsha** (respectful connection), or **Dana** (heartful offering).

Relevant Verse:

- **Chapter 3, Verse 35:**

"It is better to perform one's own duty imperfectly than to perform another's duty perfectly. By following one's own nature, one does not incur sin." (BG 3.35)

This verse highlights the importance of honoring one's own path and nature. In relationships, recognizing and respecting how others authentically express love allows us to connect with them more deeply, in alignment with their inner essence.

Similarly, understanding how people give and receive love through **Seva**, **Satya**, **Sangha**, **Sparsha**, and **Dana** helps us honor their true nature, fostering deeper personal and spiritual connections.

Relevance

- Understanding and honoring sacred expressions of love promotes mutual respect and deeper connection.
- Just as the Gita emphasizes following one's true nature, recognizing and honoring another's way of expressing love fosters authentic emotional bonds.
- Awareness of these expressions helps improve communication, reduce misunderstandings, and strengthen relationships by aligning with each person's unique spiritual and emotional preferences.

Closing Thought

Just like Sita's family learned, understanding each other's sacred expressions of love can bring more joy, connection, and understanding into your relationships.

Keep the conversation alive—truly knowing each other's hearts helps nurture deeper bonds, honor each other's nature, and cultivate love that flows selflessly and harmoniously.

Thirteen

Day 12: Respecting Boundaries

Theme

Setting and respecting boundaries with kindness, understanding, and inner balance.

Story: A Moment of Clarity

It was a warm, sunny afternoon when Raghav, Avantika's grandfather, sat on the porch, enjoying a quiet moment with his book. His daughter, Sita, had just dropped off Avantika after school. As usual, Avantika was bursting with energy, eager to spend time with her beloved grandfather.

"Grandpa, let's play a game! I missed you today!" she exclaimed, skipping toward him.

Raghav smiled at her enthusiasm but felt the weight of his responsibilities. The house had been busy lately, and his work was piling up. He glanced at the clock and realized that he needed some quiet time to finish a few tasks before dinner.

"I'd love to play with you, Avantika, but I need to finish some work right now," Raghav said, his voice soft but firm, meeting her hopeful gaze with understanding.

Avantika's face fell, a little disappointed.

"But Grandpa, you always say you're busy when I want to play!"

Raghav paused, realizing this was the perfect opportunity to honor a boundary with kindness.

"I understand that you want to spend time with me," he said, placing a hand on her shoulder. "And I love spending time with you too. But right now, I need to focus on my work. How about we play after dinner? I promise we'll have fun then."

Avantika hesitated, a little deflated but thoughtful. After a moment, she smiled.

"Okay, Grandpa, I'll wait until after dinner. We can have a special game time then!"

Raghav felt relieved, grateful for the opportunity to communicate his needs with clarity and compassion. He knew this was an important lesson for Avantika, too—that setting boundaries wasn't about rejection but about balancing needs with respect and care for each other.

That evening, after dinner, they played a game together, sharing laughter and bonding over their favorite pastime. Raghav felt grateful for both the quiet time earlier and the joyful moments that followed.

Reflection

Like Raghav, we may find ourselves needing to honor our limits and the limits of others. Boundaries are not barriers; they are a way to maintain balance between our own needs and the needs of others.

When communicated with clarity and compassion, boundaries create space for mutual respect, understanding, and harmonious connection. Acting without attachment or blame ensures that relationships remain nurturing and spiritually aligned.

Activity

Reflect

Think about a time when you honored your own boundary or respected someone else's.

- How did you feel—empowered, relieved, or maybe challenged?
- What did it teach you about your own needs or the needs of others?
- How did it feel to express or acknowledge these needs?
- What impact did it have on your relationship?

Practice

If you haven't already, consciously honor a boundary today.

- When setting a boundary:
- Speak with clarity and kindness, without blame or resentment.
- Focus on your needs in a balanced, mindful way.
- When respecting someone else's boundary:
- Acknowledge it with empathy and understanding.

- Show that you honor their needs as well as your own.

Why Boundaries Matter

- Boundaries allow us to take care of ourselves while honoring the needs of others.
- They are agreements that promote balance, not walls that separate us.
- Boundaries protect our emotional and spiritual space, ensuring we remain centered while nurturing relationships.
- When expressed with clarity and compassion, boundaries support harmony and mutual respect.

Guided by the Bhagavad Gita

The Bhagavad Gita teaches the importance of balance, moderation, and self-discipline in all aspects of life. By respecting our own needs and the needs of others, we act in a way that preserves harmony and cultivates inner peace. Setting healthy boundaries, without blame or expectation, reflects self-respect and respect for others, and aligns with the principles of equanimity (**Samatvam**) and selfless action (**Nishkama Karma**).

Relevant Verses:

- **Chapter 6, Verse 16:**
- "There is no possibility of one's becoming a yogi, O Arjuna, if one eats too much or eats too little, sleeps too much or does not sleep enough."
- **Chapter 6, Verse 17:**
- "He who is temperate in eating, recreation, working, and sleeping, who is balanced, contented, and steady in mind, is said to be a yogi,

and he is happy in this world."

These verses emphasize moderation and self-discipline as essential for inner balance and harmony. Honoring boundaries ensures that our relationships are nurtured without overstepping or neglecting our own or others' needs.

Relevance

- Boundaries protect emotional well-being and create a foundation for mutual respect and understanding.
- Just as balance is vital in yoga and life, respecting boundaries ensures that relationships remain healthy, fulfilling, and sustainable.
- Following the Gita's principle of **Samatvam** (equanimity) helps us maintain balance and harmony in relationships.
- Mindful respect for personal and others' boundaries strengthens relationships, ensuring they remain healthy, fulfilling, and spiritually aligned.

Closing Thought

Just like Raghav and Avantika learned, setting and respecting boundaries is essential for cultivating love, balance, and respect in relationships.

By practicing self-discipline and honoring the limits of ourselves and others, we create space for understanding, harmony, and deeper connection.

Fourteen

Day 13: Resolving Conflict with Discernment and Steadiness

Theme

Using the wisdom of the Bhagavad Gita to reflect on conflicts and transform them into opportunities for inner balance, understanding, and compassionate action.

Story: A Moment of Connection

It was a warm evening when Avantika and her mother, Sita, found themselves in a quiet disagreement.

Sita had asked Avantika to clean her room before they went out for dinner, but Avantika didn't want to do it just then. She had been looking forward to dinner and felt upset at the timing of her mother's request.

"I don't want to clean my room right now. I want to go to dinner!" Avantika said, frustration rising in her voice.

Sita, on the other hand, was feeling overwhelmed.

"I've asked you to do this many times, and you never listen! Why can't you just clean up?" she replied, her voice tinged with irritation.

Avantika felt her heart race, and Sita felt her patience thinning. The tension between them grew, both feeling misunderstood and unappreciated.

But in that moment, something shifted.

Sita took a deep breath, recalling the principles of **Viveka** (discernment) and **Sthitaprajna** (steady-mindedness). Instead of continuing to escalate the conflict, she reflected on her own feelings and inner state.

"I feel frustrated because I need some order and peace in the house, especially before we go out," Sita said gently. "Would you be willing to clean up for just 10 minutes so we can enjoy dinner without feeling rushed?"

Avantika's expression softened.

"I feel upset because I was really looking forward to going out, and I need some time to relax before we leave," she admitted. "Could I clean my room after we get back from dinner?"

Sita smiled, relieved that her daughter had expressed her feelings with clarity and honesty.

"That sounds like a good solution. Thank you for letting me know. Let's enjoy dinner together, and we'll sort the room afterward."

The tension lifted, and both mother and daughter walked out the door, understanding each other more deeply and feeling more connected than before.

Reflection

Like Avantika and Sita, we may find ourselves in conflict with loved ones from time to time. By practicing **discernment (Viveka)** and maintaining **steady-mindedness (Sthitaprajna)**, we can transform moments of tension into opportunities for understanding, compassion, and mutual growth.

This approach allows us to see the deeper truth in ourselves and others, fostering empathy and cooperation even in challenging situations. By focusing on our own inner state rather than assigning blame, we create space for clarity and balanced action, which strengthens relationships and heals emotional friction.

Activity

Reflect

- Think about a recent conflict or disagreement you had with someone close to you.
- How did the situation unfold?
- Did you focus on inner balance and clarity, or did you get caught in frustration and blame?

Practice

- Reflect on a recent conflict and how you might have responded using the principles of **Viveka** and **Sthitaprajna**. Consider the following steps:
- What were your feelings in the situation?
- How could you observe them without being attached or reactive?
- How could you act with clarity, compassion, and steadiness,

aligned with dharma?

Why This Matters

Practicing discernment and steady-mindedness is not about suppressing your feelings.

- It helps you respond with clarity rather than reacting impulsively.
- It fosters connection, respect, and understanding.
- It leads to more compassionate interactions.
- It transforms conflicts into opportunities for growth and harmony.

Guided by the Bhagavad Gita

The Bhagavad Gita teaches us to rise above conflict, cultivating inner steadiness and responding with wisdom and discernment (**Viveka**) and equanimity (**Sthitaprajna**). By observing situations without attachment or emotional reactivity, we act from a place of clarity and compassion rather than judgment or blame.

Relevant Verse:

- **Chapter 2, Verse 14:**
- "O son of Kunti, the nonpermanent appearance of happiness and distress, and their disappearance in due course, are like the appearance and disappearance of winter and summer seasons. They arise from sense perception, and one must learn to tolerate them without being disturbed." (BG 2.14)

This verse reminds us that external circumstances, including conflict, are temporary. By cultivating patience and detachment, we can respond thoughtfully rather than reacting impulsively.

Relevance

- Practicing non-attachment in conflict leads to peaceful resolution and greater understanding.
- Aligning with the Gita's emphasis on equanimity helps us transcend blame and emotional reactivity.
- By letting go of judgment and resentment, we release emotional burdens and respond with clarity, compassion, and wisdom.

Closing Thought

As Avantika and Sita showed us, conflicts don't have to lead to resentment.

By observing our own minds, staying balanced, and acting with discernment, we can shift from blame to understanding, transforming conflict into a space for healing and mutual growth.

This approach fosters deeper connections and helps us build relationships rooted in respect and care. It's not about being right; it's about acting in alignment with inner wisdom and dharma.

Fifteen

Day 14: Cultivating Gratitude with Devotion

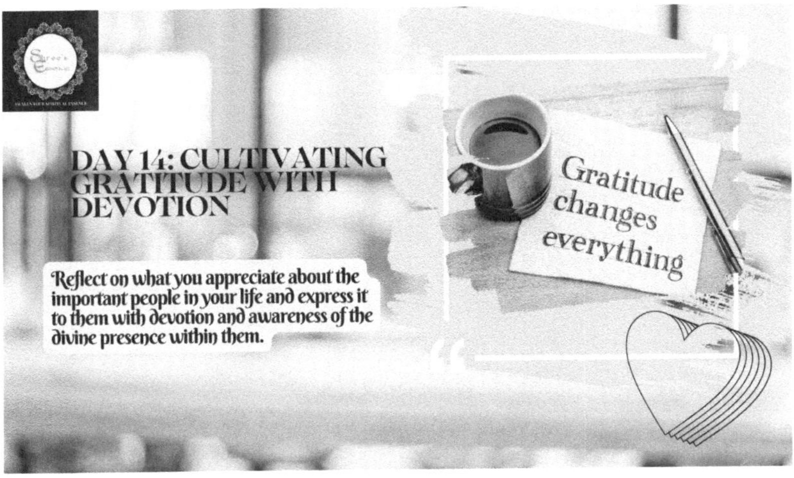

Theme

Reflect on what you appreciate about the important people in your life and express it to them with devotion and awareness of the divine presence within them.

Story: A Simple Gesture of Gratitude

It was a regular Monday evening when Avantika sat down at the dining table, scrolling through her phone while the quiet hum of the house surrounded her. Her mother, Sita, was in the kitchen, as usual, preparing dinner.

Avantika's mind was scattered with work pressures, upcoming plans, and the usual daily busyness. Yet, amidst all this, she realized something important: her mother had always been a steady source of care and support.

Sita had always been a quiet, unwavering source of love—whether it was the comforting aroma of a home-cooked meal after a long day or her soothing presence during stressful moments. But Avantika had become so used to these little gestures of love that she often took them for granted.

Today, as she watched Sita move gracefully in the kitchen, a wave of appreciation washed over Avantika.

"How often do I actually stop and thank her?" she thought, feeling a bit guilty for not expressing her gratitude sooner.

She remembered how, just last week, Sita had stayed up late helping her with a project she was stressed about, despite her own exhaustion. It was always the small things that made Avantika feel supported.

Avantika got up and walked into the kitchen, where Sita was stirring the pot. She cleared her throat before speaking.

"Mom," she began softly, "I just wanted to thank you for everything. For the way you always make sure I'm okay, for the little things like packing my lunch or checking in on me when I'm stressed. I really appreciate it."

Sita paused, looking up with a surprised yet warm smile.

"Oh, sweetheart, you don't have to thank me for that," she said, her voice gentle. "I just do it because I love you."

Avantika smiled back, feeling a warmth in her chest.

"I know, Mom. But I just wanted you to know how much it means to me. Sometimes I forget to say it, but I really do appreciate everything you do."

Sita's eyes softened, and she walked over to Avantika, pulling her into a hug.

"Thank you for saying that. It means more than you know."

In that moment, Avantika realized how important it was to express gratitude, even for the little things that are often taken for granted. A simple thank-you had deepened their connection, making her feel more bonded to her mother than ever before.

Reflection

Like Avantika, we may sometimes overlook the small acts of love and kindness in our daily lives.

Taking the time to recognize and express gratitude for these actions is an expression of **Kritajñatā** (thankfulness) and **Bhakti** (devotion)—it connects us not only with others but also with the divine essence within them.

- Gratitude nurtures understanding.
- Deepens love and enhances connection.
- Creates space for more joy, harmony, and mutual respect.

When we express appreciation, we honor the presence of the Divine (**Paramatma**) in those around us, creating an atmosphere of warmth and sacred connection in our relationships.

Activity

Reflect

Think about someone close to you—a family member, partner, or friend.

- What's one small thing they do that makes you feel loved or supported?
- It could be something they do regularly without being asked, like

checking in on you, helping with tasks, or offering emotional support.

Bhakti Practice of Gratitude

Reach out to the person you thought about in the first step.

- Express your gratitude through a heartfelt message, handwritten note, or meaningful conversation.
- Share exactly what you're grateful for and let them know how their actions make you feel.

Even a simple thank-you becomes a form of **Seva** (service) and **Yajna** (sacred offering) when offered with love and sincerity.

Why Gratitude Matters

Gratitude is a sacred attitude that transforms ordinary relationships into spiritual connections.

By regularly acknowledging the small acts that make a difference, we:

- Deepen our connections.
- Create a more positive and loving environment.
- Foster kindness, appreciation, and respect.

Expressing appreciation daily shifts our focus from lacking to abundance, from expectation to reverence, enriching our relationships and nurturing a sense of unity with all beings.

Guided by the Bhagavad Gita

Gratitude (**Kritajñatā**) is a form of **Bhakti**—a heartfelt acknowledgment of the divine presence in others.

The Bhagavad Gita teaches that gratitude is a sacred form of devotion (**Bhakti**), acknowledging the divine presence in all beings. By recognizing and appreciating the goodness and virtue in others, we honor the divine essence that flows through them.

Relevant Verse:

- **Chapter 9, Verse 22:**
- "To those who are devoted to Me and who surrender to Me with faith, I provide what they lack and preserve what they have." (BG 9.22)

This verse assures us that sincere devotion and gratitude open the heart to abundance and spiritual support. By practicing gratitude, we connect with others in a way that transcends personal desire, fostering spiritual and emotional harmony.

Relevance

- Gratitude deepens emotional bonds by acknowledging the divine in relationships.
- Fosters positive, loving, and supportive interactions.
- Shifts focus from lack to abundance, enriching our connections and cultivating unity, love, and spiritual connection with those around us.

By expressing gratitude, we awaken divine love (**Prema Bhava**) and cultivate unity, joy, and spiritual connection with those around us.

Closing Thought

Just like Avantika, you have the power to express gratitude for the everyday moments that nourish and strengthen your relationships.

Each expression of thanks deepens your connections and creates a ripple effect of positivity.

By practicing gratitude as devotion, you:

- Strengthen emotional and spiritual bonds.
- Cultivate humility and awareness of divine grace.
- Create relationships rooted in love, reverence, and joy.

A simple thank-you, offered with sincerity, becomes an act of worship.

Sixteen

Day 15: Divine Expressions of Love in Action

Theme

Strengthen your relationships by expressing appreciation through the sacred forms of love — the divine ways the Bhagavad Gita teaches us to honor the presence of the Divine in one another.

Story: Love in Action Across Generations

It was a warm Saturday morning, and the family had gathered for breakfast in the cozy dining room of Sita and Raj's home, a scene that always filled the room with a sense of belonging.

Sita, as usual, was busy in the kitchen, preparing her famous parathas for everyone, while Raj sat at the table, engrossed in the newspaper. Avantika, their daughter, sat by the window, quietly observing her family. She noticed how each person expressed love in their own unique way, and how these gestures, both big and small, created a web of connection.

Sita expressed her love through **Seva (Selfless Service)**—she had always shown love by cooking, caring, and doing thoughtful little things for her loved ones. Raj, on the other hand, expressed his love through **Satya (Truthful & Uplifting Speech)**—he often spoke words of appreciation, telling Sita how much he admired her strength and kindness.

Avantika had recently been reflecting on the Bhagavad Gita's teachings on love in action—how true love expresses itself through selflessness, truth, presence, compassion, and giving. She realized that Sita's **Seva**, though always appreciated, often went unnoticed because it was such a natural part of everyday life. Avantika wanted to express her love in a way that would truly touch her mother's heart.

That evening, she decided to ask her aunt, Urmila, for advice.

Avantika said, "Urmila, I want to show Mom how much I appreciate her, but I want it to come from the heart. What can I do?"

Urmila replied, "Your mother's love flows through Seva. She finds joy in serving everyone with love. Why don't you do something similar for her? Serve her with the same devotion she shows to all of you."

Inspired, Avantika decided to make Sita's favorite breakfast and clean up the kitchen without being asked.

The next morning, when Sita entered the kitchen, she was taken aback.

Sita exclaimed, "Avantika, you did all this?" Her voice was full of warmth and surprise.

Avantika smiled, "Yes, Mom. You always do so much for us, and I wanted to do something for you today."

Sita's eyes softened as she took the cup of chai Avantika offered her. "Thank you, darling. This means more than you know," she said.

Meanwhile, Raj, who had been watching from the corner, smiled with pride. He wanted to express his own appreciation in his way.

"Sita, you truly are the heart of this family. Your love and care hold us all together," Raj said.

Sita beamed at his words—his **Satya**, spoken with sincerity, made her feel cherished and seen.

In another corner of the home, Sita's parents, Lalitha and Raghav, reflected on their own expressions of love. Lalitha cherished **Sangha (Sacred Presence)**—spending peaceful time with her daughter—while

Raghav expressed love through **Sparsha (Respectful Connection)**—a comforting hug or a gentle touch of reassurance.

Sita asked, "Ma, shall we go for a walk together this evening?"

Lalitha replied, "I would love that! I always enjoy our walks."

Raghav, overhearing the conversation, smiled and gently placed a hand on Sita's shoulder.

"You bring joy to our home, my dear," he said softly. "A day without your smile feels incomplete."

Sita: "I know, Papa. I'm lucky to have such a loving family."

As the day continued, the family practiced expressing love in ways that resonated with each other.

Later that afternoon, Sita's close friend, Seema, stopped by with a small gift—a beautiful scarf she had picked out thoughtfully. Her gesture reflected **Dana (Heartful Offering)**—giving with love and devotion.

Sita said, "You didn't have to, Seema!"

Seema replied, "It's a small token of love. I saw it and thought of you immediately."

Sita smiled, feeling grateful for the love expressed in so many divine forms around her.

Reflection

The day's experiences were a gentle reminder that love manifests in many divine expressions.

Whether through **Satya (truthful words)**, **Seva (selfless service)**, **Sangha (mindful presence)**, **Sparsha (respectful touch)**, or **Dana (heartful giving)**, each sacred act becomes a reflection of devotion and awareness.

True love, as the Bhagavad Gita teaches, is not just in words—it is in selfless action and heartfelt intention.

When love flows without expectation, it transforms every relationship into a sacred offering.

Activity

Reflect

Think about someone close to you—a parent, partner, friend, or child.

- Which divine expression of love (Satya, Seva, Sangha, Sparsha, or Dana) do they naturally embody?
- Which of these expressions do you wish to cultivate more in your own relationships?

Divine Action

Choose one of the five expressions and practice it consciously today:

- **Satya** — Speak words that are true, kind, and uplifting.
- **Seva** — Offer selfless service with love and devotion.
- **Sangha** — Give your full presence and attention to someone.
- **Sparsha** — Offer warmth, care, and respectful affection.
- **Dana** — Share a thoughtful gift or act of generosity with gratitude.

Explanation

Each divine expression of love is a spiritual practice—a form of **Yoga in Action**.

When we embody these forms, we transform ordinary interactions into sacred connections:

- **Satya** aligns speech with truth and compassion.
- **Seva** transforms action into devotion.
- **Sangha** turns presence into meditation.
- **Sparsha** reminds us to honor divinity in others.
- **Dana** turns giving into worship.

Through these, love becomes a living expression of **Bhakti (devotion)** and **Karma Yoga (selfless action)**.

Guided by the Bhagavad Gita

The Bhagavad Gita emphasizes selfless love and action as central to spiritual and relational harmony. By expressing love according to the unique way each person receives it, we embody **Nishkama Karma**—performing acts without attachment to personal gain, while uplifting and honoring others.

Relevant Verses:

- **Chapter 3, Verse 19:**
- "Tasmād asaktaḥ satataṁ kāryaṁ karma samācara" —
- Therefore, perform your duty without attachment, for by acting without attachment one attains the Supreme.
- **Chapter 9, Verse 27:**
- "Whatever you do, whatever you eat, whatever you offer or give away, whatever austerity you perform, dedicate it to Me alone." (BG 9.27)
- **Chapter 12, Verses 13–14:**
- "One who is not envious but is a kind friend to all living beings, who is compassionate, free from possessiveness, and patient, and who has controlled mind and senses—such a devotee is dear to Me." (BG 12.13–14)
- **Chapter 6, Verse 17:**
- "He who is temperate in eating, recreation, working, and sleeping, who is balanced, contented, and steady in mind, is said to be a yogi, and he is happy in this world." (BG 6.17)

Every act of truth, service, presence, compassion, or giving becomes a spiritual offering (**Yajna**) when performed with a pure heart and without expectation. Such love uplifts both the giver and the receiver, uniting them in divine consciousness.

Relevance

- Expressing love in ways that resonate with others nurtures trust and emotional bonds.
- Fosters deep, meaningful, and spiritually aligned connections.
- Aligns relationships with the principle of selfless action (**Nishkama Karma**).
- Creates a more harmonious, compassionate, and uplifting envi-

ronment.

Why This Matters

By embodying these divine expressions of love, we:

- Nurture harmony and understanding.
- Deepen emotional and spiritual bonds.
- Live the essence of **Nishkama Karma**—acting without attachment to results.
- Create homes and relationships rooted in compassion, reverence, and joy.

Through **Satya, Seva, Sangha, Sparsha, and Dana**, love becomes not just an emotion—but a sacred practice, a living expression of the Divine within us all.

Closing Thought

When we express love through the five divine forms—Satya, Seva, Sangha, Sparsha, and Dana—we practice the art of seeing the Divine in all.

These sacred expressions deepen our relationships, bringing clarity, compassion, and unity into our hearts and homes.

Love expressed with awareness becomes devotion.

Service performed with joy becomes worship.

Presence offered with attention becomes meditation.

When we act with love aligned to the teachings of the Gita, we transform every relationship into a path toward the Divine.

Author's Note

Readers may notice that the expressions of love differ between Day 3 and Day 15, even though the characters remain the same. This variation is intentional. Each chapter draws from a specific teaching of the Bhagavad Gita and highlights a different dimension of love as it unfolds in daily life.

In Day 3, the characters appear symbolically to illustrate how various sacred expressions of love—truthful speech, selfless service, presence, respectful connection, and giving—manifest uniquely in different relationships.

In Day 15, the same characters return to show how these divine expressions of love evolve and are practiced consciously in real family interactions.

Through this continuity, readers can observe growth, reflection, and transformation across the journey—revealing that love, when guided by awareness and devotion, blossoms into both a personal and spiritual practice.

Seventeen

Day 16: Practicing Non-Judgmental Awareness

Theme

Cultivate inner balance and compassion by observing without judgment and responding with understanding.

Story: Shifting Perspectives in the Family

It was another bright morning at Sita and Raj's house. The family sat together for breakfast, but something felt off. Sita noticed Avantika was distracted, and Raj was unusually quiet. There was an unspoken tension in the air.

Avantika had been struggling with her studies, and the pressure was beginning to weigh on her. Sita, noticing her daughter's withdrawn mood, felt a wave of impatience arise within her.

"Maybe she isn't trying hard enough," she thought.

Raj, ever the observer, sensed the tension but brushed it aside. "She'll be fine. It's just a phase," he reasoned.

As the day went on, both Sita and Raj found their minds clouded with assumptions. Sita's thoughts grew critical, while Raj dismissed the situation altogether. But as evening approached, Sita recalled a verse from the Bhagavad Gita that spoke of **Samatvam Yoga Uchyate** — "**Equanimity is yoga**" (BG 2.48). She realized her judgments were disturbing her peace and preventing her from seeing the situation clearly.

Taking a deep breath, she chose stillness over reaction. Approaching Avantika with calmness, she said softly,

"Avantika, you seem a bit overwhelmed lately. Would you like to share what's on your mind?"

Avantika looked up, surprised by her mother's gentle tone. For the first time in days, she felt safe enough to speak.

"I've been finding school really hard, Ma. I'm scared to ask for help because I don't want to disappoint you," she admitted.

Sita felt her heart soften. Her earlier judgments melted away as she saw her daughter's sincerity and vulnerability. She placed a comforting hand on Avantika's shoulder.

"Thank you for sharing that with me, dear. Let's go through it together. You're not alone."

Raj, who had been listening quietly, reflected on his own detachment. He realized that true steadiness (**Sthitaprajna**) wasn't about indifference, but about balanced engagement — responding without ego or blame.

"Avantika," he said gently, "We're here to support you. Let's find a way to make things easier."

In that moment, the energy in the home shifted from judgment to understanding. The family connected in stillness, anchored in compassion rather than reaction.

Reflection

Sita felt peace returning to her heart. By letting go of assumptions and embracing awareness, she had created a space of openness and trust. Avantika, freed from the weight of fear, felt understood and supported.

Raj realized that non-judgment is not passivity — it is conscious awareness, a reflection of **Sthitaprajna (steady wisdom)** and **Samatvam (balance).**

- When we observe without judgment, we respond rather than react.
- We listen from the heart instead of the ego.
- We build understanding instead of walls.

Activity: Cultivating Non-Judgmental Awareness

Reflect

Recall a recent situation where you judged someone's behavior or words.

- What assumptions did you make?
- How did these thoughts affect your peace of mind and your connection with them?

Practice Sakshi Bhava (Witness Awareness)

Throughout the day, observe your thoughts and interactions without labeling them as right or wrong.

- If a judgment arises, pause and ask: "What truth am I not seeing right now?"
- Replace judgment with curiosity and compassion.

Respond with Balance

Next time you face a disagreement or misunderstanding, practice equanimity before responding.

- Speak gently and listen with presence.
- Let your words emerge from clarity, not reactivity.

Why Non-Judgmental Awareness Matters

When we let go of judgment, we align with the wisdom of the Bhagavad Gita. Judgment narrows the mind; awareness expands it.

- Judgment separates — awareness unites.
- Judgment reacts — awareness responds.
- Judgment clouds the intellect — awareness illuminates it.

By practicing **Sthitaprajna** and **Samatvam**, we cultivate inner peace, compassion, and understanding in all relationships.

Guided by the Bhagavad Gita

The Bhagavad Gita teaches that inner awareness and equanimity are essential for spiritual growth and harmonious relationships. By observing without judgment, we align with **Sthitaprajna** — steadiness of mind — and **Samatvam** — equanimity amidst life's circumstances.

Relevant Verses:

- **Chapter 2, Verse 48:**
- "Perform your duty with equanimity, abandoning attachment to success and failure. Such evenness of mind is called yoga."
- **Chapter 6, Verse 5:**
- Let a person uplift the self by the self; let not the self be degraded. The self is one's own friend and one's own enemy."
- **Chapter 6, Verse 8:**
- "One who is satisfied by knowledge and wisdom, steady in mind, and undisturbed by dualities — such a person is truly established in yoga."

Practicing non-judgmental awareness transforms ordinary interactions into opportunities for spiritual growth. Through **Samatvam** and **Sthitaprajna**, we learn to see others as reflections of the divine, fostering harmony, understanding, and unity.

Relevance

- Judgment creates separation, while awareness fosters unity and understanding.
- Practicing **Sakshi Bhava (witness consciousness)** allows us to observe without reacting impulsively.
- Non-judgment cultivates empathy and enables deeper, authentic connections where both individuals feel seen, valued, and understood.

When we see with awareness instead of judgment, every relationship becomes a sacred field for love, understanding, and inner evolution.

Closing Thought

True wisdom lies in seeing life without the veil of judgment. As Krishna teaches, one who remains steady amidst dualities — praise and blame, joy and sorrow — attains inner peace (BG 2.56).

By choosing awareness over judgment, you rise above the fluctuations of the mind. You begin to see others not through opinions, but through the eyes of compassion and truth.

Eighteen

Day 17: Apology and Forgiveness

Theme

Seek truth and harmony through sincere apology and compassionate forgiveness, guided by humility and inner balance.

Story: A Healing Conversation

It had been a long week, and the family had gathered for their usual weekend dinner at Raj and Sita's house. Avantika had been feeling off lately, and during dinner, a small disagreement with her mother sparked a wave of frustration.

Sita had asked Avantika to help with setting the table, but Avantika, overwhelmed with her emotions, had snapped back.

"I'm tired, Mom! Can't you ask someone else?" she said without thinking.

The words stung Sita, and the rest of the evening felt heavy. Raj, sensing the tension, decided to step in. After dinner, while the others cleaned up, he gently called Avantika aside.

"I know you're upset, sweetheart. But how you spoke to Mom didn't sound like you. What's really going on?"

Avantika lowered her eyes, her heart heavy with regret.

"I've been so overwhelmed this week, Papa. I didn't mean to speak that way. I just didn't know how to express myself. I'm really sorry."

Raj nodded understandingly.

"It's all right, Avantika. We all have difficult days. What matters is recognizing our mistakes and speaking with truth and respect. That's how we grow."

Feeling comforted, Avantika walked over to her mother, who stood quietly in the kitchen.

"Mom," she began softly, "I'm really sorry for snapping at you earlier. I was stressed, and I should have spoken more kindly. I didn't mean to hurt you."

Sita looked at her daughter with warmth. Her hurt began to dissolve as she saw the sincerity in Avantika's eyes.

"Thank you for saying that, Avantika," she replied gently. "I understand you were upset. I forgive you. What matters is that we remain truthful and kind in our hearts."

Avantika smiled with relief.

"I'll try to express myself better next time," she promised.

In that moment, both mother and daughter felt lighter. **Truth (Satya)** had dissolved misunderstanding, and **forgiveness (Kshamā)** had restored harmony.

Reflection

Like Avantika, we all face moments when our emotions take over and words escape before awareness sets in. The Bhagavad Gita reminds us that forgiveness and truthfulness are divine qualities that elevate our relationships.

When we apologize sincerely, we acknowledge **truth (Satya)** within ourselves — without ego or defensiveness. When we forgive, we release resentment and cultivate compassion (**Kshamā**). Both are acts of inner purification that strengthen our bonds and bring peace to the heart.

- Forgiveness frees both the giver and receiver.
- Sincere apology restores harmony and humility.
- Truth and compassion heal relationships and uplift the soul.

Activity: Cultivating Apology and Forgiveness

Reflect with Awareness

Think of a recent situation where tension or misunderstanding arose.

- Did pride or impatience cloud your words?
- What lesson is the divine inviting you to learn from this?

Practice Satya (Truthful Expression)

If you've hurt someone, express your apology with sincerity.

- Speak truthfully but gently.
- Focus on understanding, not justification.

Example:
"I'm sorry for my words earlier. I was stressed and lost my calm. I value our bond and will strive to communicate with more care."

Practice Kshamā (Forgiveness)

If someone approaches you with an apology, receive it with compassion.

- Let go of resentment.
- Remember that forgiveness is strength, not weakness.

Example:
"Thank you for sharing your feelings. I forgive you and appreciate your honesty."

Why Apology and Forgiveness Matter

In the Bhagavad Gita, Krishna teaches that divine qualities (**Daivi Sampat**) such as forgiveness, humility, and compassion are essential for inner and relational harmony (BG 16.3).

Apology and forgiveness are not about guilt or blame — they are spiritual disciplines. Each time we humble ourselves to seek or offer forgiveness, we dissolve the ego's grip and align closer with the Self.

- Through **Kshamā**, we release pain and anger.
- Through **Satya**, we restore clarity and truth.
- Together, they create space for understanding, unity, and unconditional love.

Guided by the Bhagavad Gita

The Bhagavad Gita teaches that forgiveness, humility, and self-control are divine qualities essential for spiritual growth and harmonious relationships. By practicing sincere apology and wholehearted forgiveness, we align our actions with **Kshamā (forgiveness)** and **Satya (truthfulness)**, dissolving resentment and cultivating inner peace.

Relevant Verse:

- **Chapter 16, Verse 3**

"Fearlessness, purity of heart, steadfastness in knowledge and yoga, charity, self-restraint, sacrifice, study of scriptures, austerity, uprightness, non-violence, truthfulness, freedom from anger, renunciation, tranquility, absence of malice, compassion, and modesty—these are the divine qualities. One who possesses them is dear to Me." (BG 16.3)

This verse highlights forgiveness (**Kshamā**), humility (**Amanitvam**), and compassion (**Dayā**) as essential qualities for dissolving conflict and nurturing relationships. Practicing apology and forgiveness reflects these divine traits and strengthens both inner and relational harmony.

Relevance

- Holding onto grievances builds barriers; forgiveness creates bridges.
- Self-inquiry (**Atma-vichara**) helps us recognize our own flaws, enabling sincere apologies and compassionate responses.
- Embracing **sattva guna** cultivates patience, understanding, and the ability to mend relationships with grace and integrity.
- Strengthens humility and self-awareness (**Amanitvam**).
- Heals emotional wounds through compassion (**Karunā**).

- Cultivates divine virtues (**Daivi Sampat**) of forgiveness and truth.
- Restores harmony in relationships through selfless communication.

By practicing **Kshamā** and **Satya**, we transform every misunderstanding into a moment of awakening — from reaction to reflection, from hurt to healing, from ego to love.

Closing Thought

When we sincerely apologize, we cleanse the heart. When we forgive, we open it to grace.

As Krishna teaches, one who practices forgiveness and humility walks the path of light and peace.

Apology and forgiveness are not mere words — they are sacred acts that dissolve separation and restore divine connection. Through **Kshamā** and **Satya**, we awaken love in its purest form: compassionate, selfless, and free from ego.

Nineteen

Day 18: Self-Compassion

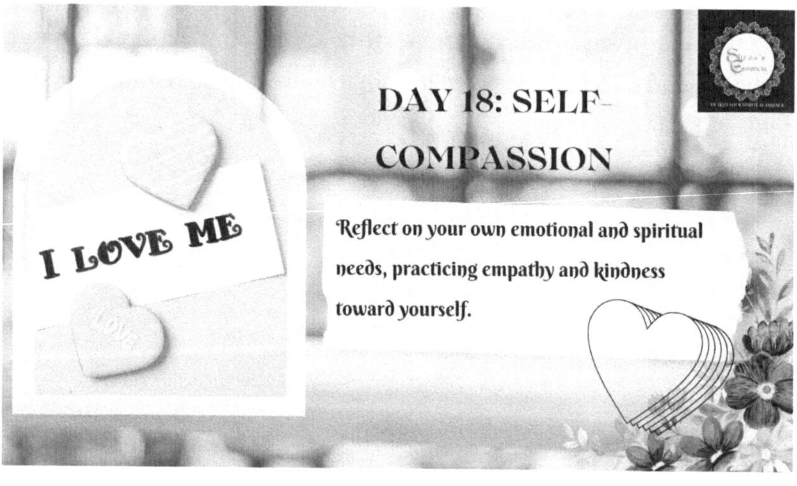

Theme

Reflect on your own emotional and spiritual needs, practicing empathy and kindness toward yourself.

Story: A Moment of Self-Compassion

It was a quiet Sunday afternoon at Raj and Sita's home. Avantika, their daughter, had spent the morning helping her grandmother, Lalitha, in the garden, and now she was sitting in the living room, feeling a bit overwhelmed. Her mother, Sita, noticed Avantika's distant gaze as she sat on the couch and approached her.

"Are you okay, Avantika? You've been so helpful today, but you seem a bit off," Sita asked gently, sitting down beside her.

Avantika hesitated for a moment. "I'm just feeling a little drained, Mom. I've been taking care of everyone, but I haven't really stopped to think about what I need."

Sita smiled kindly and placed a hand on her daughter's shoulder. "It's so easy to pour your energy into others, but it's important to recognize your own emotional needs too. You deserve the same care and kindness you give to everyone else."

Avantika nodded, realizing her mother was right. "I think I need some space to just relax and recharge, but I feel guilty for wanting that time for myself."

Sita reassured her. "Taking time for yourself isn't selfish. It's how you nurture yourself so you can be there for others with more energy and love. Self-compassion is about recognizing your needs and meeting them with kindness."

Inspired by her mother's words, Avantika closed her eyes for a moment, thinking about what she needed. "I'm going to honor my need for rest," she said softly, finally allowing herself the space to acknowledge her emotions.

Reflection

Like Avantika, we all have emotional and spiritual needs that require attention and care. Practicing self-compassion means acknowledging those needs and responding to them with kindness, just as we would for someone else. By giving ourselves the same empathy, we strengthen our inner resilience (**Atma-Vidya**) and cultivate deeper compassion (**Karunā**) for others.

Activity

Reflect

Take a moment to reflect on your emotional and spiritual needs in relationships. Ask yourself:

- What needs arise for me — space, attention, understanding, or support?
- How can I honor these needs while maintaining harmony in my relationships?

Self-Compassion Practice

Acknowledge and accept your needs without judgment. Treat yourself with the same kindness you offer to others. Ask:

- What do I need emotionally or spiritually right now?
- How can I meet that need with care, empathy, and understanding?

Why Self-Compassion Matters

Self-compassion is essential for emotional and spiritual well-being. When we recognize and respond to our own needs, we build a foundation of inner strength and self-knowledge (**Atma-Vidya**). Practicing self-compassion enables us to show up fully and authentically for others, fostering harmony, patience, and empathy in our relationships.

Guided by the Bhagavad Gita

The Bhagavad Gita emphasizes the importance of self-awareness and inner friendship. By cultivating **Atma-Vidya** (self-knowledge) and **Karunā** (compassion), we learn to care for ourselves without ego or attachment, which forms the foundation for authentic love and compassion toward others.

Relevant Verse:

- **Chapter 6, Verse 5:**

"One must elevate, not degrade, oneself with one's own mind. The mind alone is the friend of the soul, and the mind alone is the enemy of the soul." (BG 6.5)

This verse teaches that self-compassion and mindful attention to our own thoughts and emotions allow us to become our own ally. By treating ourselves with understanding and kindness, we strengthen our inner stability and spiritual growth.

Relevance

- Self-compassion is not self-indulgence; it is the foundation for inner resilience and balanced relationships.
- Awareness of our needs leads to deeper self-knowledge (**Atma-jnana**) and spiritual maturity.
- Kindness to oneself naturally cultivates compassion (**Karunā**) and empathy for others.
- Meeting our emotional and spiritual needs strengthens our ability to nurture, support, and love authentically.

Closing Thought

Self-compassion is about accepting yourself, especially in moments of vulnerability. By honoring your emotional and spiritual needs with care, you cultivate resilience, wisdom, and the capacity to love others deeply. Treat yourself with the same divine compassion (**Karunā**) that you extend to those around you.

Twenty

Day 19: Honest Sharing

Theme

Share authentic thoughts or feelings with devotion and truth, without blame or expectation.

Story: A Moment of Vulnerability

It was a quiet Sunday evening when Raj noticed his daughter Avantika sitting in the corner, her eyes distant. He had been caught up with work all afternoon and hadn't noticed how much time had passed. Now, as the family prepared for dinner, he realized he hadn't spent much time with Avantika.

"Is everything okay, sweetie?" Raj asked gently, sitting next to her.

Avantika looked up at her father. "I feel like you're always busy with work, and I don't get to spend much time with you anymore. I miss our talks," she said, her voice soft but filled with emotion.

Raj felt a pang of guilt in his heart. He had been so focused on his responsibilities that he hadn't realized how his absence affected Avantika. He took a deep breath and thought for a moment.

"I understand how you feel, Avantika," he said. "I've been caught up in work a lot, and I've missed our time together too. I need to be more present for you. Thank you for sharing that with me."

Avantika smiled softly, her feelings of hurt slowly melting away as her father acknowledged her need for connection. Raj reached out and gently hugged her, feeling the deep bond they shared.

Reflection

Honest sharing can be challenging, especially when expressing vulnerable emotions. Like Avantika, when we speak our feelings with sincerity and without blame, it opens the door for understanding and connection. By communicating from the heart, relationships are strengthened, and trust is deepened.

Activity

Reflect

Consider something you have been holding back in your relationships. It may be a feeling or need you hesitated to express. Ask yourself:

- What feeling have I been holding back?
- What need is associated with this feeling?

Honest Sharing Practice

Choose someone important in your life and share this feeling or need with them mindfully. Speak from your own experience without blaming:

- Instead of saying, "You never spend time with me," try saying, "I feel disconnected when we don't spend time together, and I need more of your presence in my life."

Why Honest Sharing Matters

Truthful and sincere communication strengthens relationships by allowing others to understand our perspective clearly. Speaking with devotion, empathy, and awareness fosters connection, trust, and emotional intimacy. Honest sharing reflects **Satya** (truthfulness) and **Shraddhā** (faithful devotion) in action, aligning our words with dharma and the well-being of all involved.

Guided by the Bhagavad Gita

Truthfulness (**Satya**) is a vital quality emphasized in Chapter 17, Verse 15, where Krishna teaches that speech should be truthful, pleasing, beneficial, and free from malice. Sharing authentically is not only about speaking the truth but doing so with awareness, devotion (**Shraddhā**), and consideration for the impact on others.

The Bhagavad Gita emphasizes the importance of purposeful and compassionate speech. By speaking with honesty (**Satya**) and sincerity of heart (**Shraddhā**), we cultivate trust, clarity, and harmony in relationships. Words should uplift, heal, and reflect awareness of the divine essence in ourselves and others.

Relevant Verse:

- Chapter 17, Verse 15:
- "That which is truthful, pleasing, and beneficial; which is not agitating to others; that is said to be the austerity of speech." (BG 17.15)

This verse highlights that truthful expression should be compassionate and considerate, fostering understanding rather than causing harm. Honest sharing guided by devotion transforms communication into a sacred act.

Relevance

- Speaking authentically nurtures trust, reduces misunderstandings, and strengthens bonds.
- Aligning words with dharma ensures honesty promotes connection instead of conflict.
- Sharing with awareness and empathy creates a safe space for meaningful dialogue and spiritual connection.
- Practicing **Satya** in our words cultivates integrity, devotion, and harmonious relationships.

Closing Thought

Like Avantika, you too can experience the healing power of honest sharing. By speaking your truth with compassion and devotion, you cultivate understanding, emotional closeness, and meaningful connection in your relationships.

Twenty-One

Day 20: Celebrating Sacred Connections

Theme

Plan an enjoyable activity with a loved one to honor your bond through devotion (Bhakti) and selfless service (Seva).

Story: A Bond Strengthened

It was a sunny afternoon, and Avantika had been feeling a bit down lately. Her mother, Sita, had been busy with household duties and preparing for the upcoming family gathering. Avantika knew how much her mother had on her plate, but she couldn't help feeling neglected. She missed the moments when they would spend time together—just the two of them.

Sita noticed her daughter's quiet demeanor and walked into the living room, sitting beside her.

"Avantika, you seem a bit distant today. Is everything okay?"

Avantika hesitated. "I've just been feeling a little left out, Mom. I know you're busy, but I miss the times we used to spend together baking or doing something fun."

Sita's heart softened. She realized that in the midst of her busy schedule, she had unintentionally neglected Avantika's need for presence and attention. Gently taking her daughter's hand, she said,

"I'm really sorry, sweetheart. You're so important to me, and I'd never want you to feel that way."

Avantika looked up with understanding. "It's okay, Mom. I just really miss our time together."

Sita smiled warmly. "Let's change that. How about we take a break from everything and do something together today? I'll make time for you, I promise."

Together, they decided to bake cookies, just like old times. As they worked side by side in the kitchen, Sita gave Avantika her undivided attention. They laughed, shared stories, and enjoyed each other's company, fully immersed in the moment.

"I'm so glad we're doing this, Mom," Avantika said, her face lighting up with happiness.

Sita smiled, feeling a deep sense of connection. "Me too, sweetheart. Thank you for reminding me how important this time is."

In that simple yet meaningful activity, their bond was rekindled, and both Sita and Avantika felt a renewed sense of closeness and love.

Reflection

Celebrating connections is about making time for those we love, honoring their needs, and expressing love through devotion (Bhakti) and selfless attention (Seva). When we intentionally connect in this way, we cultivate deeper, more meaningful relationships.

Activity

Reflect:

Think about someone important to you—whether a partner, child, parent, or friend. How can you give them your presence, attention, and care today?

Celebration Activity:

Plan a meaningful activity to honor your connection. Express your love through:

- **Seva (Selfless Service):** Offer help or support with sincerity and without expectation.
- **Sangha / Presence:** Spend mindful, uninterrupted time together.
- **Sparsha / Compassionate Touch:** Share a caring gesture, like a hug or gentle presence.
- **Satya / Truthful Words:** Speak with honesty, kindness, and appreciation.

Why Celebrating Connections Matters

Honoring and celebrating relationships strengthens emotional and spiritual bonds. By practicing devotion and selfless attention, we recognize the sacredness in every connection, fostering love, trust, and closeness.

Guided by the Bhagavad Gita

The Bhagavad Gita teaches that the divine essence resides in all beings, and recognizing this sacred unity nurtures devotion (Bhakti) and selfless service (Seva). By celebrating our connections, we honor both the divine within others and the sacred bond we share.

Relevant Verse:

- Chapter 9, Verse 29:
- "I am equal to all beings. Those who see Me in all and all in Me, with equal vision, truly recognize the divine unity." (BG 9.29)

Krishna speaks of honoring the divine presence in all beings in Chapter 9, Verse 29, declaring that he is equally present in everyone. Those who see with **sama-darshana** (equal vision) recognize this sacred unity. Celebrating our connections means seeing them as divine gifts and cherishing them with gratitude, devotion, and selfless attention.

Relevance

- By expressing **Bhakti** (devotion) and **Seva** (selfless service) in our relationships, we strengthen sacred bonds and cultivate spiritual growth. Every relationship, when honored with reverence, becomes a path to self-discovery and divine connection.
- Honoring relationships acknowledges their role in our personal and spiritual growth.
- Expressing bhakti through appreciation, gratitude, and joyful interaction strengthens bonds.
- Recognizing every relationship as a divine gift transforms everyday

connections into a path for self-discovery and divine connection.

Closing Thought

When we celebrate the connections we share, we nurture and deepen our relationships. Acts of devotion and care, no matter how small, create lasting memories and remind us of the divine presence in the people we cherish.

Twenty-Two

Day 21: Reflection on Growth

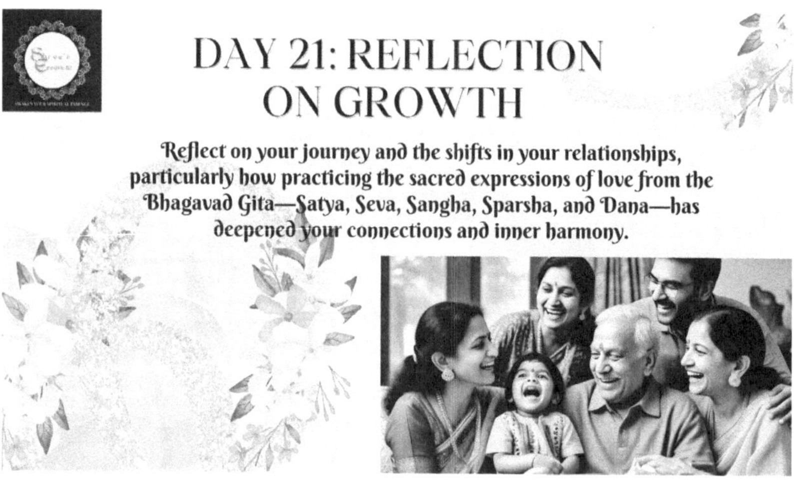

Theme

Reflect on your journey and the shifts in your relationships, particularly how practicing the sacred expressions of love from the Bhagavad Gita—Satya, Seva, Sangha, Sparsha, and Dana—has deepened your connections and inner harmony.

Story: A Family Reflection

It was a beautiful Sunday afternoon when Sita decided to bring the whole family together for a special conversation. She had been reflecting on the changes in her relationships over the past few weeks, especially through practicing the sacred expressions of love taught in the Bhagavad Gita. She knew this was the perfect opportunity to connect with each family member, understand their hearts, and strengthen their bonds.

Sita gathered Raj (her husband), Avantika (her daughter), Lalitha and Raghav (her parents), Seema (her best friend), and Urmila (her younger sister) in the living room. Each person sat comfortably, ready to listen and share. Sita began by expressing her gratitude for the growth they had all experienced together.

"I've been reflecting a lot on how we express our love and attention to each other," Sita said with a warm smile. "Through devotion (Bhakti), selfless service (Seva), truthful and uplifting speech (Satya), mindful presence (Sangha), compassionate touch (Sparsha), and heartful giving (Dana), I've seen our relationships transform. I want to hear from all of you: How can we continue to connect deeply and nurture our bonds?"

Raj, always practical, spoke first.

"I've realized that performing acts of Seva with love makes me feel connected and fulfilled. I see how offering help or supporting each other with selfless intention strengthens our bonds. I want to continue being mindful in serving others without expectation."

Avantika, who had been listening eagerly, shared her heart.

"I feel most loved when you speak with Satya—truthful, kind, and uplifting words. It makes me feel seen and cherished. I also want to cultivate the patience to understand others' ways of expressing love, even when they are different from mine."

Lalitha, Sita's mother, added gently,

"For me, spending mindful time together—Sangha—is what deepens my sense of connection. When we are fully present with each other, even for a short while, I feel joy and harmony."

Raghav, Sita's father, nodded thoughtfully.

"I realize that I need to practice Sparsha more consciously—not just physical touch, but compassionate presence. Being aware and attentive strengthens our emotional and spiritual closeness."

Seema, Sita's best friend, smiled and spoke,

"I've learned that Dana, giving with devotion, even in small ways, creates joy. Simple acts of generosity remind me of the sacredness of our connections, and I want to express this more often."

Urmila, Sita's younger sister, added,

"For me, mindful attention and presence—Sangha—combined with affectionate Sparsha, bring the most comfort. I see how small gestures of care nurture our bonds and bring harmony."

The conversation flowed naturally, with each person reflecting on how they could express love in ways that resonate with the teachings of the Bhagavad Gita. They celebrated the shifts in their communication and the ways they had grown closer through devotion, service, truthful speech, mindful presence, compassionate touch, and heartful giving.

"I'm so proud of how much we've grown together," Sita said. "By practicing these sacred expressions of love, our relationships have strengthened. We are learning to listen, care, and connect in ways that truly matter."

Reflection

Growth in relationships is a gradual process. By expressing love through Satya, Seva, Sangha, Sparsha, and Dana, we nurture deeper understanding, empathy, and harmony. Reflection allows us to notice the subtle shifts in our hearts and in our interactions, reinforcing inner stability (Sthitaprajna) and the path of self-study (Svadhyaya).

Activity

Reflect:

- Take a moment to notice how your relationships have evolved through practicing the sacred expressions of love.

- Observe how your attention, actions, words, and presence have impacted those around you.
- Consider how devotion (Bhakti) and selfless action (Seva) have strengthened bonds.

Writing:

- Write down reflections on the ways your practice of Satya, Seva, Sangha, Sparsha, and Dana has influenced your relationships.
- Note areas of growth and opportunities to cultivate more awareness and presence.
- Capture insights from your family or loved ones that can guide further personal and relational growth.

Why These Practices Matter

The Bhagavad Gita teaches that love expressed through truthfulness, devotion, selfless service, mindful presence, compassionate touch, and generosity creates trust, understanding, and spiritual connection. When we act with awareness of the divine in ourselves and others, relationships become pathways to self-realization and inner harmony.

Guided by the Bhagavad Gita

The Bhagavad Gita emphasizes self-reflection (Svadhyaya) as essential for spiritual and personal growth. By reviewing our actions, thoughts, and interactions, we cultivate inner stability (Sthitaprajna) and awareness of how our efforts in love, compassion, and presence have influenced our relationships.

Relevant Verse:

- Chapter 6, Verse 5:
- "One must elevate, not degrade, oneself with one's own mind. The mind alone is the friend of the soul, and the mind alone is the enemy of the soul." (BG 6.5)

This verse teaches that introspection and mindful reflection help us recognize our progress and refine our actions, leading to greater harmony and alignment with our spiritual purpose.

Relevance

- Reflection fosters self-awareness, gratitude, and recognition of personal and relational growth.
- Conscious review strengthens our commitment to inner development (atma-vikas) and spiritual alignment.
- Observing the evolution of our connections encourages mindful living and deepens the practice of love, compassion, and presence in everyday life.

Closing Thought

Growth in relationships is a journey, not a destination. Each conscious expression of love nurtures harmony, deepens bonds, and brings joy to all involved. Just as Sita and her family reflected on their journey, you can continue to observe, celebrate, and cultivate sacred expressions of love in your own life.

Twenty-Three

Glossary of Key Terms and Concepts

Atma-Vidya (Self-Knowledge / Self-Compassion)

The awareness and understanding of your own mind, heart, and spiritual needs. Practicing Atma-Vidya involves offering kindness and care to oneself, recognizing your inherent worth, and cultivating inner balance.

Bhakti (Devotion / Heartful Connection)

A loving, devoted approach to life and relationships. Bhakti emphasizes honoring the divine in all beings through gratitude, love, and selfless actions.

Dana (Heartful Offering / Generosity)

Giving freely from the heart, without expectation of reward. Small acts of generosity—like words of encouragement, gestures of care, or shared resources—deepen love and strengthen bonds.

Karunā (Compassion / Empathy)

The ability to feel and respond to others' emotions with understanding and kindness. Practicing Karunā nurtures patience, forgiveness, and emotional connection within relationships.

Kritajñatā (Gratitude / Appreciation)

Acknowledging and expressing thankfulness for the presence, actions, and qualities of others. Gratitude fosters trust, reinforces bonds, and encourages positive interactions.

Kshamā (Forgiveness / Letting Go)

The conscious choice to release resentment or anger toward others or oneself. Kshamā allows relationships to heal and encourages resilience and harmony.

Nishkama Karma (Selfless Action / Acting Without Attachment)

Performing one's duties or acts of service without expecting personal gain or reward. This principle cultivates humility, generosity, and genuine love in action.

Samatvam (Equanimity / Non-Judgmental Awareness)

Maintaining balance in thoughts, emotions, and actions, regardless of external circumstances. Samatvam allows one to respond with clarity, patience, and fairness.

Samādhi (Steadfast Awareness / Inner Balance)

A state of calm, focused attention, and equanimity. While not explicitly listed as a separate day, it underlies practices like Samatvam, Sthitaprajna, and Sankalpa.

Sankalpa (Intention / Resolve)

A conscious decision or inner resolve to act mindfully and purposefully. It guides presence, attention, and deliberate action in relationships.

Satya (Truthful Speech / Honesty in Communication)

Speaking truthfully, kindly, and constructively. Satya encourages authentic expression while avoiding harm, fostering trust and open communication.

Sangha (Sacred Presence / Mindful Time Together)

Being fully present and attentive in shared moments, whether in conversation, play, or rituals. Sangha nurtures connection and emotional intimacy.

Seva (Selfless Service / Acts of Love)

Offering help, support, or care without seeking reward or recognition. Seva strengthens bonds, models humility, and reinforces the value of service in relationships.

Sparsha (Respectful Connection / Compassionate Touch)

Engaging with others with awareness, respect, and care. Sparsha reflects the recognition of the divine or sacred in each person and promotes gentle, loving interactions.

Shraddhā (Faithful Attention / Devoted Listening)

Listening with full attention, presence, and sincerity. Shraddhā fosters understanding, validates experiences, and strengthens trust in relationships.

Svadhyaya (Self-Reflection / Personal Growth)

Observing and reflecting on one's thoughts, actions, and emotions. Svadhyaya supports conscious behavior, accountability, and continuous growth in relationships and self-development.

Sthitaprajna (Steadfastness / Inner Stability)

Maintaining composure, patience, and clarity regardless of circumstances. Sthitaprajna builds trust, reliability, and resilience in relationships.

Viveka (Discernment / Wise Understanding)

The ability to evaluate situations, understand needs, and make balanced choices. Viveka encourages thoughtful action and compassionate responses in challenging circumstances.

Twenty-Four

Conclusion

The teachings of the Bhagavad Gita guide us to embody:

Satya (Truthful & Uplifting Speech), **Seva** (Selfless Service), **Sangha** (Sacred Presence), **Sparsha** (Respectful Connection), **Dana** (Heartful Offering), **Kshamā** (Forgiveness), **Kritajñatā** (Gratitude), **Samatvam** (Equanimity), **Sthitaprajna** (Steadfastness), **Karunā** (Compassion), **Shraddhā** (Faithful Attention), **Viveka** (Discernment), **Svadhyaya** (Self-Reflection), and **Nishkama Karma** (Selfless Action).

Living these principles nurtures deeper relationships, inner harmony, and a life of purpose, meaning, and fulfillment.

1. Satya (Truthful & Uplifting Speech)

BG 17.14–16 – Austerity of Speech, Eating, Work, and Recreation

- **BG 17.14:** "The austerity of speech consists in speaking words that are truthful, pleasing, and beneficial; words that do not cause distress to others and are in accordance with dharma and spiritual discipline."

- **BG 17.15:** "The austerity of eating consists of consuming food that is pure, wholesome, and agreeable, which sustains life, strength, health, happiness, and satisfaction. Eating in moderation, without overindulgence, is part of this discipline."
- **BG 17.16:** "The austerity of work and recreation consists in engaging in activities with self-discipline, without attachment or disturbance to others, and in a way that maintains balance, cleanliness, and devotion. Work and enjoyment done in this manner purify the mind and heart."

Relevance: Speaking truthfully, kindly, and beneficially strengthens trust and emotional safety within the family. Mindful and disciplined habits in eating, work, and recreation model balance for children and partners, fostering harmony, inner peace, and a nurturing household. Using language that uplifts encourages positive dialogue, reduces misunderstandings, and deepens love in relationships.

2. Seva (Selfless Service / Nishkama Karma)

- **BG 2.47:** "You have a right to work only, but never to its fruits. Let not the fruits of action be your motive, nor let your attachment be to inaction."
- **BG 3.19:** "Therefore, without being attached to the fruits of activities, one should act as a matter of duty, for by working without attachment, one attains the Supreme."

Relevance: Performing selfless service within the family—helping with household chores, supporting a partner, or attending to children without expecting praise—cultivates humility, mutual respect, and stronger bonds. It models service-oriented love and teaches family members that acts of care and devotion are fulfilling in themselves, fostering a supportive, cooperative home environment.

3. Sangha (Sacred Presence / Mindful Time)

BG 6.10–15:

- **Verse 6.10:** "One should sit in a clean spot and practice yoga, keeping the body, head, and neck erect, steady, and motionless, and focusing the mind in meditation."
- **Verse 6.11:** "Let the yogi perform regulated duties, be moderate in eating and recreation, and work without attachment, keeping the mind free from agitation."
- **Verse 6.12:** "Yoga is the steady control of the mind and senses, free from desire and restlessness; the yogi is satisfied in self, and finds contentment within."
- **Verse 6.13:** "Thus, practicing moderation in sleep, food, work, and recreation, the yogi attains balance and steadiness in mind."
- **Verse 6.14–15:** "By controlling the mind and senses and remaining focused in meditation, the yogi becomes free from agitation and achieves inner calm. Such a balanced and focused mind leads to true peace, contentment, and steady awareness."

Relevance: Being fully present with family members—during meals, conversations, play, or shared rituals—deepens emotional intimacy and strengthens bonds. Mindful presence demonstrates care and attention, reducing feelings of neglect or disconnection. Practicing steady awareness, moderation, and balance helps family members approach one another with calmness, patience, and receptivity, creating a safe and loving environment.

4. Sparsha (Respectful Connection / Compassion / Ahimsa)

- **BG 6.30:** "He who sees Me everywhere and sees all beings in Me, I am never lost to him, nor is he ever lost to Me."

Relevance: Recognizing the inherent divinity in each family member nurtures compassion and respect, allowing members to approach disagreements with understanding rather than judgment. This awareness encourages gentle communication, forgiveness, and non-harming, strengthening authentic connections and creating a family culture of empathy and acceptance.

5. Dana (Heartful Offering / Generosity)

- **BG 9.26:** "If one offers Me with love a leaf, a flower, a fruit, or water, I accept it."

Relevance: Simple acts of love—like preparing a favorite meal, offering a comforting word, or sharing a thoughtful gesture—express devotion and strengthen family bonds. Heartful giving models generosity and gratitude for children, reinforces emotional connection among spouses, and honors the sacredness of everyday family interactions.

6. Kshamā (Forgiveness)

- **BG 16.3:** "Humility, modesty, non-violence, forgiveness, uprightness, service to guru, purity, steadfastness, self-control, and renunciation of the objects of desire—these are the divine qualities."

Relevance: Forgiveness dissolves resentment, heals emotional wounds, and restores harmony within family relationships. By practicing forgiveness, parents model conflict resolution for children, partners rebuild trust, and household interactions become more compassionate and peaceful. Forgiveness strengthens resilience, allowing families to grow through challenges together.

7. Kritajñatā (Gratitude / Appreciation)

- **BG 12.13–14:** "He who is free from malice toward all beings, friendly and compassionate, free from possessiveness and ego, content, steady in meditation, and engaged in selfless work—such a devotee is dear to Me."
- **BG 9.22:** "To those who dedicate themselves with faith and devotion, I provide all that is necessary and protect them."

Relevance: Expressing gratitude—thanking family members for support, care, and presence—reinforces trust, strengthens emotional bonds, and nurtures a loving environment. Gratitude encourages mutual appreciation, reduces ego-driven conflicts, and helps family members recognize the divine qualities in one another, cultivating harmony and connection.

8. Samatvam (Equanimity / Balance / Non-Judgment)

- **BG 2.14:** "O son of Kunti, the dualities of pleasure and pain are temporary. Endure them with equanimity; they do not last forever."
- **BG 6.5:** "One must elevate, not degrade, oneself with one's own mind. The mind alone is the friend of the soul, and the mind alone is the enemy of the soul."

- **BG 6.16–17:** Krishna advises moderation in eating, sleeping, work, and recreation, avoiding extremes to maintain inner balance.

Relevance: Equanimity allows family members to respond calmly to stress, disagreements, and challenging situations. Practicing balance in speech, actions, and emotions reduces reactive behavior, fosters understanding, and encourages compassionate resolution of conflicts. It also models emotional regulation for children, creating a stable and harmonious household.

9. Sthitaprajna (Steadfastness / Inner Stability)

- **BG 6.5:** Emphasizes self-mastery: the mind can either uplift or degrade us; disciplined awareness builds inner stability.

Relevance: Steadfastness and inner stability create trust and reliability in family relationships. When parents or partners maintain composure and self-mastery, family members feel secure, supported, and guided. This quality fosters resilience in relationships and encourages consistent, loving engagement even during stressful times.

10. Karunā (Compassion / Empathy)

- **BG 5.18:** "The humble sage, by true knowledge, sees equally a learned brahmana, a cow, an elephant, a dog, and even one who eats dog meat."

Relevance: Compassion helps family members understand each other's emotions, perspectives, and challenges. It reduces judgment, promotes patience, and strengthens empathy across generations. Children learn to care for others, partners navigate challenges with kindness, and the family becomes a safe space for emotional expression and support.

11. Shraddhā (Faithful Attention / Devoted Listening)

- **BG 2.11 onward:** Arjuna listens attentively to Krishna's teachings, demonstrating presence, openness, and devotion.
- **BG 2.70:** "A person with a mind disciplined like the ocean, steady and undisturbed, attains inner peace."

Relevance: Attentive listening strengthens trust, demonstrates respect, and validates the experiences of family members. It allows for meaningful dialogue, reduces misunderstandings, and encourages openness. Devoted attention in family interactions promotes emotional intimacy, reinforces bonds, and nurtures a supportive, caring environment.

12. Viveka (Discernment / Understanding Needs / Reflection on Conflict)

- **BG 2.13:** "As the soul experiences childhood, youth, and old age in the body, so does it take on new bodies in succession."
- **BG 3.35:** "Better to follow one's own dharma than to imitate another's; performing one's own duty imperfectly is better than another's duty well."
- **BG 2.14:** Dualities of pleasure and pain are temporary, helping discern right action without being swayed by emotion.

Relevance: Discernment allows family members to navigate conflicts wisely, understand each other's needs, and respond thoughtfully rather than reactively. It promotes healthy boundaries, respects individual differences, and encourages choices aligned with both personal and collective wellbeing. Applying discernment strengthens harmony and trust in relationships.

13. Svadhyaya (Self-Reflection / Personal Growth)

- **BG 6.5:** Self-awareness is crucial for elevating the mind, fostering personal growth, and deepening understanding of oneself and others.

Relevance: Reflecting on one's behavior, words, and attitudes promotes conscious engagement with family members. Self-reflection encourages accountability, improves communication, and nurtures emotional intelligence, making relationships more compassionate and resilient. It supports ongoing personal and collective growth within the family.

14. Nishkama Karma (Selfless Action / Acting Without Attachment)

- **BG 2.47:** "You have a right to perform your prescribed duties, but you are not entitled to the fruits of your actions. Never consider yourself the cause of the results of your activities, and never be attached to not doing your duty."
- **BG 3.19:** "Therefore, without being attached to the results of activities, one should perform work as a matter of duty, for by working without attachment, one attains the Supreme."

Relevance: Performing family responsibilities selflessly—without expecting recognition or reward—builds trust, strengthens connections, and creates a loving and cooperative home environment. It teaches children the value of service, fosters mutual support among adults, and aligns family life with spiritual principles of love and harmony.

Epilogue

As you close this book, remember that relationships are alive — they grow, shift, and evolve with time. They require patience, attention, and the courage to meet others — and ourselves — with honesty, compassion, and devotion. The teachings of the Bhagavad Gita are not a destination but a path, guiding us to act selflessly, speak truthfully, reflect sincerely, and honor the divine presence in all beings.

I offer my heartfelt gratitude to every individual who participated in the workshop — your openness and engagement were the seeds that have now blossomed into this book. May the insights and practices shared here inspire you to bring awareness, compassion, and devotion into your daily life. May you cultivate harmony in your home, serenity in your heart, and courage to navigate challenges with equanimity.

Above all, may this book remind you that every act of love, no matter how small, is a step on the path of spiritual growth, and that the sacred is often found in the everyday moments of connection.

— Vijayshree

Afterword

Love, in its truest essence, is not bound by form, word, or time.

The Bhagavad Gita teaches us that love is the soul's expression — a sacred flow that connects all beings through awareness, compassion, and selfless service.

Each of the *Five Sacred Expressions of Love*—

- **Satya** (Truthful and uplifting speech),
- **Seva** (Selfless service),
- **Sangha** (Mindful presence),
- **Sparsha** (Respectful human connection), and
- **Dana** (Heartful offering)—

is a living prayer, a practice that transforms ordinary interactions into acts of devotion.

Through *Satya*, our words become gentle vessels of truth and healing.

Through *Seva*, our actions turn into worship, free from attachment.

Through *Sangha*, our presence becomes meditation, allowing love to be felt in silence.

Through *Sparsha,* our touch carries reverence, seeing the divine in every being.

Through *Dana,* our giving becomes gratitude, reflecting abundance from within.

When these five expressions guide our relationships, love is no longer conditional—it becomes conscious, steady, and luminous. The Gita reminds us that when actions, words, and intentions flow from purity of heart, they become yoga—union with the Divine.

This book is an offering from my heart — born from life's simple moments of love, misunderstanding, forgiveness, and rediscovery. Coming from a large joint family, I have seen love expressed in countless ways — sometimes through words, sometimes through silence. It is from those sacred spaces that these reflections took shape.

May these teachings remind you that love is already within you — waiting to be expressed through your truth, service, presence, touch, and giving.

When lived with awareness, every act becomes sacred, every relationship becomes a mirror of the soul, and every moment becomes a step toward divine connection.

With gratitude and light,

Vijayshree Ratanparkhe

About the Author

Vijayshree Ratanparkhe's journey with spirituality has been deeply rooted in everyday life, growing up in a large joint family where love, challenges, and togetherness were experienced in abundance. From a young age, she felt a quiet connection with the divine, which later blossomed into a lifelong exploration of the **Bhagavad Gita**.

Through the Gita, Vijayshree discovered that love is not just an emotion—it is a conscious practice, expressed through truth, service, presence, compassion, and selfless giving. These timeless teachings inspired her to translate spiritual wisdom into practical guidance for nurturing relationships, strengthening bonds, and deepening understanding between people.

Her writing reflects real-life dynamics, drawing on the joys, conflicts, and tender moments of family life, while integrating the transformative principles of the Gita. In this book, she explores the *Five Sacred Expressions of Love*—**Satya, Seva, Sangha, Sparsha, and Dana**—showing how these spiritual practices can enrich everyday interactions, foster empathy, and cultivate harmony in the heart and home.

Some of her guiding verses from the Bhagavad Gita include:

"Perform your duty without attachment to its fruits." (2.47)

"The yogi dwells in steady awareness and calm, controlling the mind and senses." (6.10–15)

"One who sees Me in all, and all in Me, is never separated from Me." (6.30)

"Offer even a leaf, a flower, a fruit, or water to Me with devotion; this offering reaches Me." (9.26)

Through this book, Vijayshree hopes to inspire readers to express love consciously, honor each person's unique nature, and build relationships that reflect both compassion and spiritual awareness—reminding us that every act of love is also a step toward inner growth and connection with the Divine.

You can connect with me on:

https://shreesessencia.com

https://x.com/Vijayshreerp

https://www.facebook.com/shreesessencia

https://www.linkedin.com/in/vijayshree-r-48024aa6

Also by Vijayshree R

Vijayshree Ratanparkhe is a spiritual guide, author, and workshop facilitator whose work bridges the timeless wisdom of the Bhagavad Gita with practical guidance for personal growth, emotional well-being, and purposeful living. Her writing focuses on **transforming human experiences into actionable insights**, helping readers recognize their inner challenges, awaken self-awareness, and live a life of clarity, balance, and fulfillment.

Her previous books include:

Avantika's Train to Truth – The Journey to Your Life's Purpose

Life's journey is rarely a straight track—it bends, halts, and challenges us to choose who we will become. In *Avantika's Train to Truth,* a young woman faces obstacles that force her to question everything she knows. With courage as her ticket and the Bhagavad Gita as her compass, she learns how to turn doubt into direction and struggle into purpose. Inspiring and deeply relatable, this story invites every reader to board their own train toward truth, clarity, and fulfillment.

When Children Forget, Life Remembers - A journey of healing for parents left behind

Every parent gives everything to their children—but what remains when the nest empties and love seems forgotten? *When Children Forget, Life Remembers* traces Jagdish and Lalitha's journey from heartbreak to healing. Guided by the Bhagavad Gita, they discover that emptiness is not an ending, but an invitation to deeper love and higher purpose. Gentle, wise, and universal, this story reminds us that love rooted in the soul never disappears—it only changes form.

21 Days to Emotional and Spiritual Detox

Are you ready to transform your mind, heart, and life? *21 Days to Emotional and Spiritual Detox* draws on the timeless wisdom of the Bhagavad Gita to guide you in purifying thoughts, actions, and emotional patterns. This book helps you overcome the six inner impurities—lust, anger, greed, pride, envy, and delusion—and cultivate lasting personal and spiritual growth. Practical exercises, reflections, and daily practices make ancient wisdom accessible, helping readers reclaim clarity, balance, and harmony in daily life.

9 789334 451634

Printed at Repro India Ltd.